50 United Kingdom Ice Cream Recipes for Home

By: Kelly Johnson

Table of Contents

- Vanilla Ice Cream
- Chocolate Ice Cream
- Strawberry Ice Cream
- Cookies and Cream Ice Cream
- Mint Chocolate Chip Ice Cream
- Coffee Ice Cream
- Rocky Road Ice Cream
- Butter Pecan Ice Cream
- Cookie Dough Ice Cream
- Peanut Butter Cup Ice Cream
- Cherry Garcia Ice Cream
- Neapolitan Ice Cream
- Pistachio Ice Cream
- Black Raspberry Ice Cream
- S'mores Ice Cream
- Key Lime Pie Ice Cream
- Birthday Cake Ice Cream
- Banana Pudding Ice Cream
- Caramel Swirl Ice Cream
- Mocha Almond Fudge Ice Cream
- Coconut Ice Cream
- Red Velvet Ice Cream
- Lemon Sorbet
- Orange Sherbet
- Peach Ice Cream
- Blueberry Cheesecake Ice Cream
- Apple Pie Ice Cream
- Snickerdoodle Ice Cream
- Maple Walnut Ice Cream
- Pumpkin Pie Ice Cream
- Eggnog Ice Cream
- Rum Raisin Ice Cream
- Toffee Crunch Ice Cream
- Honeycomb Ice Cream
- Almond Joy Ice Cream

- Salted Caramel Pretzel Ice Cream
- Cinnamon Roll Ice Cream
- White Chocolate Macadamia Nut Ice Cream
- Bourbon Pecan Pie Ice Cream
- Grape Nut Ice Cream
- Buttermilk Ice Cream
- Avocado Ice Cream
- Matcha Green Tea Ice Cream
- Caramelized Banana Ice Cream
- Pina Colada Ice Cream
- Peanut Butter and Jelly Ice Cream
- Coconut Lime Ice Cream
- Honey Lavender Ice Cream
- Blackberry Cobbler Ice Cream
- Bacon Maple Ice Cream

Vanilla Ice Cream

Ingredients:

- 2 cups heavy cream
- 1 cup whole milk
- 3/4 cup granulated sugar
- Pinch of salt
- 1 vanilla bean, split lengthwise (or 1 tablespoon vanilla extract)
- 4 large egg yolks

Instructions:

1. In a saucepan, combine the heavy cream, whole milk, half of the sugar, and pinch of salt. If using a vanilla bean, scrape the seeds into the mixture and add the pod too. Heat over medium heat, stirring occasionally, until the mixture is hot and just begins to bubble around the edges. Do not let it boil.
2. In a separate bowl, whisk the egg yolks with the remaining sugar until pale and slightly thickened.
3. Gradually pour about half of the hot cream mixture into the egg yolks, whisking constantly, to temper the yolks.
4. Pour the tempered egg mixture back into the saucepan with the remaining cream mixture. Cook over medium-low heat, stirring constantly, until the custard thickens slightly and coats the back of a spoon (about 170-175°F or 77-80°C). Do not let it boil.
5. Remove the saucepan from heat and stir in the vanilla extract if using instead of the vanilla bean.
6. Strain the custard through a fine-mesh sieve into a clean bowl to remove the vanilla bean pod and any bits of cooked egg.
7. Cover the bowl with plastic wrap, pressing it directly onto the surface of the custard to prevent a skin from forming. Chill in the refrigerator for at least 4 hours or overnight.
8. Once chilled, churn the Vanilla custard in an ice cream maker according to the manufacturer's instructions until it reaches a soft-serve consistency.
9. Transfer the churned ice cream to a freezer-safe container, press a piece of parchment paper or plastic wrap directly onto the surface, and freeze until firm (usually 4-6 hours).
10. Serve the Vanilla Ice Cream scooped into bowls or cones, topped with fresh berries or your favorite toppings.

Enjoy the creamy, pure flavor of homemade Vanilla Ice Cream! This recipe makes about 1 quart of ice cream. Adjust sweetness and vanilla intensity according to your preference for the perfect scoop.

Chocolate Ice Cream

Ingredients:

- 2 cups heavy cream
- 1 cup whole milk
- 3/4 cup granulated sugar
- Pinch of salt
- 6 ounces semi-sweet or dark chocolate, finely chopped (about 1 cup)
- 4 large egg yolks
- 1 teaspoon vanilla extract

Instructions:

1. In a saucepan, combine the heavy cream, whole milk, half of the sugar, and pinch of salt. Heat over medium heat, stirring occasionally, until the mixture is hot and just begins to bubble around the edges. Do not let it boil.
2. Place the finely chopped chocolate in a heatproof bowl.
3. In a separate bowl, whisk the egg yolks with the remaining sugar until pale and slightly thickened.
4. Gradually pour about half of the hot cream mixture into the egg yolks, whisking constantly, to temper the yolks.
5. Pour the tempered egg mixture back into the saucepan with the remaining cream mixture. Cook over medium-low heat, stirring constantly, until the custard thickens slightly and coats the back of a spoon (about 170-175°F or 77-80°C). Do not let it boil.
6. Immediately pour the hot custard over the chopped chocolate. Let it sit for a minute to melt the chocolate, then stir until smooth and well combined.
7. Stir in the vanilla extract.
8. Strain the chocolate custard through a fine-mesh sieve into a clean bowl to remove any bits of cooked egg or chocolate pieces.
9. Cover the bowl with plastic wrap, pressing it directly onto the surface of the custard to prevent a skin from forming. Chill in the refrigerator for at least 4 hours or overnight.
10. Once chilled, churn the Chocolate custard in an ice cream maker according to the manufacturer's instructions until it reaches a soft-serve consistency.
11. Transfer the churned ice cream to a freezer-safe container, press a piece of parchment paper or plastic wrap directly onto the surface, and freeze until firm (usually 4-6 hours).

12. Serve the Chocolate Ice Cream scooped into bowls or cones, topped with chocolate sauce or chocolate shavings if desired.

Enjoy the rich and indulgent flavor of homemade Chocolate Ice Cream! This recipe makes about 1 quart of ice cream. Adjust sweetness by varying the amount of sugar used, depending on the bitterness of your chocolate and your preference for sweetness.

Strawberry Ice Cream

Ingredients:

- 1 pound fresh strawberries, hulled and chopped
- 1 cup granulated sugar, divided
- 2 cups heavy cream
- 1 cup whole milk
- Pinch of salt
- 4 large egg yolks
- 1 teaspoon vanilla extract

Instructions:

1. **Prepare the strawberries:**
     - In a bowl, combine the chopped strawberries with 1/2 cup of sugar. Stir well and let them sit at room temperature for about 30 minutes to macerate, releasing their juices.
2. **Make the ice cream base:**
     - In a saucepan, combine the heavy cream, whole milk, remaining 1/2 cup of sugar, and pinch of salt. Heat over medium heat, stirring occasionally, until the mixture is hot and just begins to bubble around the edges. Do not let it boil.
3. **Temper the eggs:**
     - In a separate bowl, whisk the egg yolks until smooth. Gradually pour about half of the hot cream mixture into the egg yolks, whisking constantly, to temper the yolks.
4. **Combine the custard:**
     - Pour the tempered egg mixture back into the saucepan with the remaining cream mixture. Cook over medium-low heat, stirring constantly, until the custard thickens slightly and coats the back of a spoon (about 170-175°F or 77-80°C). Do not let it boil.
5. **Blend the strawberries:**
     - Transfer the macerated strawberries and their juices into a blender or food processor. Blend until smooth. You can strain the mixture through a fine-mesh sieve if you prefer a smoother texture.
6. **Incorporate the flavors:**
     - Remove the custard from heat and stir in the vanilla extract.
     - Stir the strawberry puree into the custard until well combined.
7. **Chill the custard:**

- Strain the strawberry custard through a fine-mesh sieve into a clean bowl to remove any bits of cooked egg or strawberry seeds.
- Cover the bowl with plastic wrap, pressing it directly onto the surface of the custard to prevent a skin from forming. Chill in the refrigerator for at least 4 hours or overnight.

8. **Churn and freeze:**
   - Once chilled, churn the Strawberry custard in an ice cream maker according to the manufacturer's instructions until it reaches a soft-serve consistency.
9. **Final freezing:**
   - Transfer the churned ice cream to a freezer-safe container, press a piece of parchment paper or plastic wrap directly onto the surface, and freeze until firm (usually 4-6 hours).
10. **Serve:**
    - Serve the Strawberry Ice Cream scooped into bowls or cones, garnished with fresh strawberries or a drizzle of strawberry sauce if desired.

Enjoy the fresh and fruity flavors of homemade Strawberry Ice Cream! This recipe makes about 1 quart of ice cream. Adjust sweetness by varying the amount of sugar used, depending on the sweetness of your strawberries and your personal preference.

Cookies and Cream Ice Cream

Ingredients:

- 2 cups heavy cream
- 1 cup whole milk
- 3/4 cup granulated sugar
- Pinch of salt
- 1 teaspoon vanilla extract
- 15-20 chocolate sandwich cookies (like Oreo cookies), coarsely chopped

Instructions:

1. In a saucepan, combine the heavy cream, whole milk, half of the sugar, and pinch of salt. Heat over medium heat, stirring occasionally, until the mixture is hot and just begins to bubble around the edges. Do not let it boil.
2. In a separate bowl, whisk the egg yolks with the remaining sugar until pale and slightly thickened.
3. Gradually pour about half of the hot cream mixture into the egg yolks, whisking constantly, to temper the yolks.
4. Pour the tempered egg mixture back into the saucepan with the remaining cream mixture. Cook over medium-low heat, stirring constantly, until the custard thickens slightly and coats the back of a spoon (about 170-175°F or 77-80°C). Do not let it boil.
5. Remove the saucepan from heat and stir in the vanilla extract.
6. Strain the custard through a fine-mesh sieve into a clean bowl to remove any bits of cooked egg.
7. Cover the bowl with plastic wrap, pressing it directly onto the surface of the custard to prevent a skin from forming. Chill in the refrigerator for at least 4 hours or overnight.
8. Once chilled, churn the vanilla custard in an ice cream maker according to the manufacturer's instructions until it reaches a soft-serve consistency.
9. During the last few minutes of churning, add the chopped cookies into the ice cream maker, allowing them to mix evenly throughout the ice cream.
10. Transfer the churned Cookies and Cream Ice Cream to a freezer-safe container, press a piece of parchment paper or plastic wrap directly onto the surface, and freeze until firm (usually 4-6 hours).
11. Serve the Cookies and Cream Ice Cream scooped into bowls or cones, garnished with extra cookie crumbs if desired.

Enjoy the classic taste of homemade Cookies and Cream Ice Cream, perfect for any occasion! This recipe makes about 1 quart of ice cream. Adjust sweetness and cookie amount according to your preference for the ideal creamy texture and cookie crunch.

Mint Chocolate Chip Ice Cream

Ingredients:

- 2 cups heavy cream
- 1 cup whole milk
- 3/4 cup granulated sugar
- Pinch of salt
- 2 teaspoons peppermint extract (adjust to taste)
- Green food coloring (optional)
- 1 cup chocolate chips or chopped chocolate (semisweet or dark, according to preference)

Instructions:

1. In a saucepan, combine the heavy cream, whole milk, half of the sugar, and pinch of salt. Heat over medium heat, stirring occasionally, until the mixture is hot and just begins to bubble around the edges. Do not let it boil.
2. In a separate bowl, whisk the egg yolks with the remaining sugar until pale and slightly thickened.
3. Gradually pour about half of the hot cream mixture into the egg yolks, whisking constantly, to temper the yolks.
4. Pour the tempered egg mixture back into the saucepan with the remaining cream mixture. Cook over medium-low heat, stirring constantly, until the custard thickens slightly and coats the back of a spoon (about 170-175°F or 77-80°C). Do not let it boil.
5. Remove the saucepan from heat and stir in the peppermint extract. Add green food coloring if desired, a few drops at a time, until you achieve the desired shade of mint.
6. Strain the custard through a fine-mesh sieve into a clean bowl to remove any bits of cooked egg.
7. Cover the bowl with plastic wrap, pressing it directly onto the surface of the custard to prevent a skin from forming. Chill in the refrigerator for at least 4 hours or overnight.
8. Once chilled, churn the Mint custard in an ice cream maker according to the manufacturer's instructions until it reaches a soft-serve consistency.
9. During the last few minutes of churning, add the chocolate chips or chopped chocolate into the ice cream maker, allowing them to mix evenly throughout the ice cream.

10. Transfer the churned Mint Chocolate Chip Ice Cream to a freezer-safe container, press a piece of parchment paper or plastic wrap directly onto the surface, and freeze until firm (usually 4-6 hours).
11. Serve the Mint Chocolate Chip Ice Cream scooped into bowls or cones, garnished with extra chocolate chips if desired.

Enjoy the refreshing and chocolatey flavors of homemade Mint Chocolate Chip Ice Cream! This recipe makes about 1 quart of ice cream. Adjust the amount of peppermint extract and chocolate according to your taste preference for the perfect balance of minty freshness and chocolate richness.

Coffee Ice Cream

Ingredients:

- 2 cups heavy cream
- 1 cup whole milk
- 3/4 cup granulated sugar
- Pinch of salt
- 1/2 cup coarsely ground coffee beans (or instant coffee powder, to taste)
- 4 large egg yolks
- 1 teaspoon vanilla extract

Instructions:

1. In a saucepan, combine the heavy cream, whole milk, half of the sugar, salt, and coarsely ground coffee beans. Heat over medium heat, stirring occasionally, until the mixture is hot and just begins to bubble around the edges. Do not let it boil.
2. Remove the saucepan from heat, cover it, and let the mixture steep for about 30 minutes to infuse the coffee flavor. If using instant coffee powder, skip this steeping process and proceed directly to the next step.
3. Strain the coffee-infused cream mixture through a fine-mesh sieve into a clean saucepan, pressing on the coffee grounds to extract as much liquid as possible. Discard the coffee grounds.
4. In a separate bowl, whisk the egg yolks with the remaining sugar until pale and slightly thickened.
5. Gradually pour about half of the hot coffee-infused cream mixture into the egg yolks, whisking constantly, to temper the yolks.
6. Pour the tempered egg mixture back into the saucepan with the remaining cream mixture. Cook over medium-low heat, stirring constantly, until the custard thickens slightly and coats the back of a spoon (about 170-175°F or 77-80°C). Do not let it boil.
7. Remove the saucepan from heat and stir in the vanilla extract.
8. Strain the custard through a fine-mesh sieve into a clean bowl to remove any bits of cooked egg.
9. Cover the bowl with plastic wrap, pressing it directly onto the surface of the custard to prevent a skin from forming. Chill in the refrigerator for at least 4 hours or overnight.
10. Once chilled, churn the Coffee custard in an ice cream maker according to the manufacturer's instructions until it reaches a soft-serve consistency.

11. Transfer the churned Coffee Ice Cream to a freezer-safe container, press a piece of parchment paper or plastic wrap directly onto the surface, and freeze until firm (usually 4-6 hours).
12. Serve the Coffee Ice Cream scooped into bowls or cones, garnished with chocolate-covered coffee beans or a drizzle of caramel if desired.

Enjoy the rich and aromatic flavors of homemade Coffee Ice Cream! This recipe makes about 1 quart of ice cream. Adjust the amount of coffee according to your taste preference for a stronger or milder coffee flavor.

Rocky Road Ice Cream

Ingredients:

- 2 cups heavy cream
- 1 cup whole milk
- 3/4 cup granulated sugar
- Pinch of salt
- 1 teaspoon vanilla extract
- 1/2 cup unsweetened cocoa powder
- 1/2 cup mini marshmallows
- 1/2 cup chopped nuts (such as almonds, pecans, or walnuts)
- 4 ounces semi-sweet chocolate, chopped (optional, for extra chocolatey flavor)

Instructions:

1. In a saucepan, combine the heavy cream, whole milk, half of the sugar, salt, and cocoa powder. Heat over medium heat, stirring occasionally, until the mixture is hot and just begins to bubble around the edges. Do not let it boil.
2. In a separate bowl, whisk the egg yolks with the remaining sugar until pale and slightly thickened.
3. Gradually pour about half of the hot cocoa-infused cream mixture into the egg yolks, whisking constantly, to temper the yolks.
4. Pour the tempered egg mixture back into the saucepan with the remaining cream mixture. Cook over medium-low heat, stirring constantly, until the custard thickens slightly and coats the back of a spoon (about 170-175°F or 77-80°C). Do not let it boil.
5. Remove the saucepan from heat and stir in the vanilla extract.
6. Strain the custard through a fine-mesh sieve into a clean bowl to remove any bits of cocoa powder or cooked egg.
7. Cover the bowl with plastic wrap, pressing it directly onto the surface of the custard to prevent a skin from forming. Chill in the refrigerator for at least 4 hours or overnight.
8. Once chilled, churn the Rocky Road custard in an ice cream maker according to the manufacturer's instructions until it reaches a soft-serve consistency.
9. During the last few minutes of churning, add the mini marshmallows, chopped nuts, and chopped chocolate (if using) into the ice cream maker, allowing them to mix evenly throughout the ice cream.

10. Transfer the churned Rocky Road Ice Cream to a freezer-safe container, press a piece of parchment paper or plastic wrap directly onto the surface, and freeze until firm (usually 4-6 hours).
11. Serve the Rocky Road Ice Cream scooped into bowls or cones, garnished with extra mini marshmallows and chopped nuts if desired.

Enjoy the rich chocolate flavor and delightful textures of homemade Rocky Road Ice Cream! This recipe makes about 1 quart of ice cream. Adjust the amount of marshmallows, nuts, and chocolate according to your taste preference for the perfect balance of flavors and textures.

Butter Pecan Ice Cream

Ingredients:

- 1 cup pecan halves
- 4 tablespoons unsalted butter
- 2 cups heavy cream
- 1 cup whole milk
- 3/4 cup granulated sugar
- Pinch of salt
- 4 large egg yolks
- 1 teaspoon vanilla extract

Instructions:

1. **Toast the pecans:**
   - Preheat your oven to 350°F (175°C). Spread the pecan halves in a single layer on a baking sheet and toast them in the oven for 8-10 minutes, or until fragrant and lightly browned. Watch them closely to prevent burning. Remove from the oven and let them cool completely. Once cooled, roughly chop the toasted pecans.
2. **Prepare the buttered pecans:**
   - In a skillet or saucepan, melt the butter over medium heat. Add the chopped pecans and stir to coat them evenly with butter. Cook for 3-5 minutes, stirring frequently, until the pecans are toasted and fragrant. Remove from heat and let them cool completely.
3. **Make the ice cream base:**
   - In a saucepan, combine the heavy cream, whole milk, half of the sugar, and pinch of salt. Heat over medium heat, stirring occasionally, until the mixture is hot and just begins to bubble around the edges. Do not let it boil.
4. **Temper the eggs:**
   - In a separate bowl, whisk the egg yolks with the remaining sugar until pale and slightly thickened.
   - Gradually pour about half of the hot cream mixture into the egg yolks, whisking constantly, to temper the yolks.
5. **Combine the custard:**
   - Pour the tempered egg mixture back into the saucepan with the remaining cream mixture. Cook over medium-low heat, stirring constantly, until the

custard thickens slightly and coats the back of a spoon (about 170-175°F or 77-80°C). Do not let it boil.

6. **Add vanilla and pecans:**
   - Remove the saucepan from heat and stir in the vanilla extract.
   - Stir in the cooled buttered pecans, reserving a handful for topping if desired.
7. **Chill the custard:**
   - Strain the custard through a fine-mesh sieve into a clean bowl to remove any bits of cooked egg or pecan pieces.
   - Cover the bowl with plastic wrap, pressing it directly onto the surface of the custard to prevent a skin from forming. Chill in the refrigerator for at least 4 hours or overnight.
8. **Churn and freeze:**
   - Once chilled, churn the Butter Pecan custard in an ice cream maker according to the manufacturer's instructions until it reaches a soft-serve consistency.
9. **Final freezing:**
   - Transfer the churned Butter Pecan Ice Cream to a freezer-safe container, press a piece of parchment paper or plastic wrap directly onto the surface, and sprinkle with reserved chopped pecans if desired. Freeze until firm (usually 4-6 hours).
10. **Serve:**
    - Serve the Butter Pecan Ice Cream scooped into bowls or cones, garnished with extra toasted pecans if desired.

Enjoy the creamy, nutty goodness of homemade Butter Pecan Ice Cream! This recipe makes about 1 quart of ice cream. Adjust sweetness and nuttiness according to your preference for a delightful ice cream experience.

Cookie Dough Ice Cream

Ingredients:

For the cookie dough:

- 1/2 cup unsalted butter, softened
- 1/4 cup granulated sugar
- 1/2 cup packed light brown sugar
- 2 tablespoons milk
- 1/2 teaspoon vanilla extract
- 1 cup all-purpose flour
- 1/4 teaspoon salt
- 1/2 cup mini chocolate chips

For the ice cream base:

- 2 cups heavy cream
- 1 cup whole milk
- 3/4 cup granulated sugar
- Pinch of salt
- 1 teaspoon vanilla extract

Instructions:

1. **Make the cookie dough:**
    - In a mixing bowl, cream together the softened butter, granulated sugar, and brown sugar until light and fluffy.
    - Mix in the milk and vanilla extract.
    - Gradually add the flour and salt, mixing until combined.
    - Stir in the mini chocolate chips until evenly distributed.
    - Shape the cookie dough into small balls or pieces and place them on a parchment-lined baking sheet. Freeze until firm, about 1-2 hours.
2. **Prepare the ice cream base:**
    - In a saucepan, combine the heavy cream, whole milk, half of the sugar, and pinch of salt. Heat over medium heat, stirring occasionally, until the mixture is hot and just begins to bubble around the edges. Do not let it boil.
3. **Temper the eggs:**
    - In a separate bowl, whisk the egg yolks with the remaining sugar until pale and slightly thickened.

- Gradually pour about half of the hot cream mixture into the egg yolks, whisking constantly, to temper the yolks.
4. **Combine the custard:**
    - Pour the tempered egg mixture back into the saucepan with the remaining cream mixture. Cook over medium-low heat, stirring constantly, until the custard thickens slightly and coats the back of a spoon (about 170-175°F or 77-80°C). Do not let it boil.
5. **Chill the custard:**
    - Remove the saucepan from heat and stir in the vanilla extract.
    - Strain the custard through a fine-mesh sieve into a clean bowl to remove any bits of cooked egg.
6. **Chill the custard:**
    - Cover the bowl with plastic wrap, pressing it directly onto the surface of the custard to prevent a skin from forming. Chill in the refrigerator for at least 4 hours or overnight.
7. **Churn the ice cream:**
    - Once chilled, churn the vanilla custard in an ice cream maker according to the manufacturer's instructions until it reaches a soft-serve consistency.
8. **Add cookie dough chunks:**
    - During the last few minutes of churning, add the frozen cookie dough chunks into the ice cream maker, allowing them to mix evenly throughout the ice cream.
9. **Final freezing:**
    - Transfer the churned Cookie Dough Ice Cream to a freezer-safe container, pressing a piece of parchment paper or plastic wrap directly onto the surface, and freeze until firm (usually 4-6 hours).
10. **Serve:**
    - Serve the Cookie Dough Ice Cream scooped into bowls or cones, enjoying the delicious chunks of cookie dough in every bite.

Enjoy the creamy and chunky goodness of homemade Cookie Dough Ice Cream! This recipe makes about 1 quart of ice cream. Adjust sweetness and cookie dough amount according to your preference for the perfect cookie dough to ice cream ratio.

Peanut Butter Cup Ice Cream

Ingredients:

- 2 cups heavy cream
- 1 cup whole milk
- 3/4 cup granulated sugar
- Pinch of salt
- 1 teaspoon vanilla extract
- 1/2 cup creamy peanut butter
- 1/2 cup chopped peanut butter cups (about 8-10 mini peanut butter cups)

Instructions:

1. **Prepare the ice cream base:**
    - In a saucepan, combine the heavy cream, whole milk, half of the sugar, and pinch of salt. Heat over medium heat, stirring occasionally, until the mixture is hot and just begins to bubble around the edges. Do not let it boil.
2. **Mix the peanut butter mixture:**
    - In a separate bowl, whisk together the creamy peanut butter and remaining sugar until well combined and smooth.
3. **Temper the eggs:**
    - Gradually pour about half of the hot cream mixture into the peanut butter mixture, whisking constantly, to temper it.
4. **Combine and cook:**
    - Pour the tempered peanut butter mixture back into the saucepan with the remaining cream mixture. Cook over medium-low heat, stirring constantly, until the custard thickens slightly and coats the back of a spoon (about 170-175°F or 77-80°C). Do not let it boil.
5. **Add vanilla extract:**
    - Remove the saucepan from heat and stir in the vanilla extract.
6. **Chill the custard:**
    - Strain the custard through a fine-mesh sieve into a clean bowl to remove any bits of peanut butter.
7. **Cool and churn:**
    - Cover the bowl with plastic wrap, pressing it directly onto the surface of the custard to prevent a skin from forming. Chill in the refrigerator for at least 4 hours or overnight.

- Once chilled, churn the peanut butter custard in an ice cream maker according to the manufacturer's instructions until it reaches a soft-serve consistency.
8. **Add peanut butter cups:**
    - During the last few minutes of churning, add the chopped peanut butter cups into the ice cream maker, allowing them to mix evenly throughout the ice cream.
9. **Final freezing:**
    - Transfer the churned Peanut Butter Cup Ice Cream to a freezer-safe container, press a piece of parchment paper or plastic wrap directly onto the surface, and freeze until firm (usually 4-6 hours).
10. **Serve:**
    - Serve the Peanut Butter Cup Ice Cream scooped into bowls or cones, topped with extra chopped peanut butter cups if desired.

Enjoy the creamy peanut butter flavor and chocolatey chunks of homemade Peanut Butter Cup Ice Cream! This recipe makes about 1 quart of ice cream. Adjust the amount of peanut butter and peanut butter cups according to your taste preference for the perfect balance of flavors.

Cherry Garcia Ice Cream

Ingredients:

- 2 cups heavy cream
- 1 cup whole milk
- 3/4 cup granulated sugar
- Pinch of salt
- 1 teaspoon vanilla extract
- 1 cup pitted and chopped cherries (fresh or frozen)
- 1/2 cup chocolate chunks or chopped chocolate (dark or semisweet)

Instructions:

1. **Prepare the ice cream base:**
    - In a saucepan, combine the heavy cream, whole milk, half of the sugar, and pinch of salt. Heat over medium heat, stirring occasionally, until the mixture is hot and just begins to bubble around the edges. Do not let it boil.
2. **Cherries preparation:**
    - While the cream mixture is heating, prepare the cherries by pitting and chopping them into small pieces. If using frozen cherries, thaw and drain excess liquid.
3. **Temper the eggs:**
    - In a separate bowl, whisk the egg yolks with the remaining sugar until pale and slightly thickened.
    - Gradually pour about half of the hot cream mixture into the egg yolks, whisking constantly, to temper the yolks.
4. **Combine and cook:**
    - Pour the tempered egg mixture back into the saucepan with the remaining cream mixture. Cook over medium-low heat, stirring constantly, until the custard thickens slightly and coats the back of a spoon (about 170-175°F or 77-80°C). Do not let it boil.
5. **Add vanilla extract and chill:**
    - Remove the saucepan from heat and stir in the vanilla extract.
    - Strain the custard through a fine-mesh sieve into a clean bowl to remove any bits of cooked egg.
6. **Cool and churn:**

- Stir in the chopped cherries. Cover the bowl with plastic wrap, pressing it directly onto the surface of the custard to prevent a skin from forming. Chill in the refrigerator for at least 4 hours or overnight.
- Once chilled, churn the Cherry Garcia custard in an ice cream maker according to the manufacturer's instructions until it reaches a soft-serve consistency.

7. **Add chocolate chunks:**
    - During the last few minutes of churning, add the chocolate chunks into the ice cream maker, allowing them to mix evenly throughout the ice cream.
8. **Final freezing:**
    - Transfer the churned Cherry Garcia Ice Cream to a freezer-safe container, press a piece of parchment paper or plastic wrap directly onto the surface, and freeze until firm (usually 4-6 hours).
9. **Serve:**
    - Serve the Cherry Garcia Ice Cream scooped into bowls or cones, enjoying the delicious blend of cherries and chocolate in every bite.

Enjoy the homemade goodness of Cherry Garcia Ice Cream! This recipe makes about 1 quart of ice cream. Adjust the sweetness and chocolate ratio according to your taste preference for the perfect balance of flavors.

Neapolitan Ice Cream

Ingredients:

For each flavor (Vanilla, Chocolate, and Strawberry):

Vanilla Ice Cream:

- 1 cup heavy cream
- 1 cup whole milk
- 1/2 cup granulated sugar
- Pinch of salt
- 1 teaspoon vanilla extract

Chocolate Ice Cream:

- 1 cup heavy cream
- 1 cup whole milk
- 1/2 cup granulated sugar
- Pinch of salt
- 1/4 cup unsweetened cocoa powder

Strawberry Ice Cream:

- 1 cup heavy cream
- 1 cup whole milk
- 1/2 cup granulated sugar
- Pinch of salt
- 1 cup fresh strawberries, hulled and chopped (or frozen strawberries, thawed)

Instructions:

Vanilla Ice Cream:

1. In a saucepan, combine the heavy cream, whole milk, half of the sugar, and pinch of salt. Heat over medium heat, stirring occasionally, until the mixture is hot and just begins to bubble around the edges. Do not let it boil.
2. Remove from heat and stir in the vanilla extract.
3. Strain the mixture through a fine-mesh sieve into a clean bowl to remove any bits of cooked egg or vanilla bean pods.

4. Cover the bowl with plastic wrap, pressing it directly onto the surface of the custard to prevent a skin from forming. Chill in the refrigerator for at least 4 hours or overnight.
5. Once chilled, churn the Vanilla custard in an ice cream maker according to the manufacturer's instructions until it reaches a soft-serve consistency.
6. Transfer the churned Vanilla Ice Cream to a freezer-safe container, press a piece of parchment paper or plastic wrap directly onto the surface, and freeze until firm (usually 4-6 hours).

Chocolate Ice Cream:

1. Follow the same steps as for Vanilla Ice Cream, but add the cocoa powder to the cream mixture in step 1. Whisk well to combine before heating.
2. Continue with steps 2-6 as described for Vanilla Ice Cream.

Strawberry Ice Cream:

1. In a blender or food processor, puree the strawberries until smooth.
2. In a saucepan, combine the heavy cream, whole milk, half of the sugar, and pinch of salt. Heat over medium heat, stirring occasionally, until the mixture is hot and just begins to bubble around the edges. Do not let it boil.
3. Remove from heat and stir in the pureed strawberries.
4. Strain the mixture through a fine-mesh sieve into a clean bowl to remove any pulp or seeds.
5. Cover the bowl with plastic wrap, pressing it directly onto the surface of the custard to prevent a skin from forming. Chill in the refrigerator for at least 4 hours or overnight.
6. Once chilled, churn the Strawberry custard in an ice cream maker according to the manufacturer's instructions until it reaches a soft-serve consistency.
7. Transfer the churned Strawberry Ice Cream to a freezer-safe container, press a piece of parchment paper or plastic wrap directly onto the surface, and freeze until firm (usually 4-6 hours).

Assembly:

1. Once all three flavors (Vanilla, Chocolate, and Strawberry) are firm, you can assemble them in layers in a freezer-safe container, alternating between flavors.
2. For the classic Neapolitan style, create horizontal layers of Vanilla, Chocolate, and Strawberry.

3. Press a piece of parchment paper or plastic wrap directly onto the surface of the ice cream and freeze until firm (usually 4-6 hours).
4. Serve the Neapolitan Ice Cream scooped into bowls or cones, enjoying the classic trio of flavors!

This recipe makes about 1 quart of each flavor, enough to create a traditional Neapolitan Ice Cream block with distinct layers. Adjust sweetness and intensity of flavors according to your preference for a delightful homemade treat.

Pistachio Ice Cream

Ingredients:

- 2 cups heavy cream
- 1 cup whole milk
- 3/4 cup granulated sugar
- Pinch of salt
- 1 cup shelled pistachios (unsalted, preferably roasted)
- 1 teaspoon vanilla extract
- 4 large egg yolks

Instructions:

1. **Prepare the pistachios:**
   - Place the pistachios in a food processor or blender and process until finely ground. Set aside a small amount of finely ground pistachios for garnish, if desired.
2. **Make the custard base:**
   - In a saucepan, combine the heavy cream, whole milk, sugar, and salt. Heat over medium heat, stirring occasionally, until the mixture is hot and begins to steam, but do not let it boil.
3. **Infuse the pistachios:**
   - Add the ground pistachios to the hot cream mixture and remove the saucepan from heat. Let it steep for about 30 minutes to allow the flavors to meld. Strain the mixture through a fine-mesh sieve into a clean bowl to remove the pistachio solids.
4. **Temper the eggs:**
   - In a separate bowl, whisk the egg yolks until smooth. Gradually whisk in about half of the hot cream mixture into the egg yolks to temper them.
5. **Combine and cook:**
   - Pour the egg yolk mixture back into the saucepan with the remaining cream mixture. Cook over medium-low heat, stirring constantly with a wooden spoon or spatula, until the custard thickens slightly and coats the back of the spoon (about 170-175°F or 77-80°C). Do not let it boil.
6. **Finish the custard:**
   - Remove the saucepan from heat and stir in the vanilla extract. Let the custard cool to room temperature, then cover and refrigerate for at least 4 hours or overnight.
7. **Churn the ice cream:**

- Once the custard is thoroughly chilled, churn it in an ice cream maker according to the manufacturer's instructions until it reaches a soft-serve consistency.

8. **Freeze the ice cream:**
   - Transfer the churned Pistachio Ice Cream to a freezer-safe container. Sprinkle the reserved finely ground pistachios over the top, if using. Press a piece of parchment paper or plastic wrap directly onto the surface of the ice cream to prevent ice crystals from forming.

9. **Set and serve:**
   - Freeze the ice cream until firm, usually 4-6 hours. Serve the Pistachio Ice Cream scooped into bowls or cones, enjoying its creamy texture and nutty flavor.

Enjoy your homemade Pistachio Ice Cream! This recipe makes about 1 quart. Feel free to adjust the sweetness or nutty intensity to suit your taste.

Black Raspberry Ice Cream

Ingredients:

- 2 cups heavy cream
- 1 cup whole milk
- 3/4 cup granulated sugar
- Pinch of salt
- 1 teaspoon vanilla extract
- 1 cup fresh or frozen black raspberries (thawed if frozen)
- 1 tablespoon lemon juice
- 4 large egg yolks

Instructions:

1. **Prepare the black raspberries:**
   - In a blender or food processor, puree the black raspberries until smooth. Strain through a fine-mesh sieve to remove seeds, if desired. Stir in the lemon juice and set aside.
2. **Make the custard base:**
   - In a saucepan, combine the heavy cream, whole milk, sugar, and salt. Heat over medium heat, stirring occasionally, until the mixture is hot and begins to steam, but do not let it boil.
3. **Temper the eggs:**
   - In a separate bowl, whisk the egg yolks until smooth. Gradually whisk in about half of the hot cream mixture into the egg yolks to temper them.
4. **Combine and cook:**
   - Pour the egg yolk mixture back into the saucepan with the remaining cream mixture. Cook over medium-low heat, stirring constantly with a wooden spoon or spatula, until the custard thickens slightly and coats the back of the spoon (about 170-175°F or 77-80°C). Do not let it boil.
5. **Add vanilla and raspberry puree:**
   - Remove the saucepan from heat and stir in the vanilla extract.
   - Stir in the black raspberry puree until well combined.
6. **Chill the custard:**
   - Strain the custard through a fine-mesh sieve into a clean bowl to remove any bits of cooked egg or raspberry seeds.
   - Cover the bowl with plastic wrap, pressing it directly onto the surface of the custard to prevent a skin from forming. Chill in the refrigerator for at least 4 hours or overnight.

7. **Churn the ice cream:**
   - Once the custard is thoroughly chilled, churn it in an ice cream maker according to the manufacturer's instructions until it reaches a soft-serve consistency.
8. **Freeze the ice cream:**
   - Transfer the churned Black Raspberry Ice Cream to a freezer-safe container. Press a piece of parchment paper or plastic wrap directly onto the surface of the ice cream to prevent ice crystals from forming.
9. **Set and serve:**
   - Freeze the ice cream until firm, usually 4-6 hours. Serve the Black Raspberry Ice Cream scooped into bowls or cones, enjoying its fruity flavor and creamy texture.

Enjoy your homemade Black Raspberry Ice Cream! This recipe makes about 1 quart. Adjust the sweetness or tartness by adding more or less sugar depending on your taste preference.

S'mores Ice Cream

Ingredients:

- 2 cups heavy cream
- 1 cup whole milk
- 3/4 cup granulated sugar
- Pinch of salt
- 1 teaspoon vanilla extract
- 1/2 cup mini marshmallows
- 1/2 cup crushed graham crackers
- 1/2 cup chocolate chunks or chips

Instructions:

1. **Prepare the ice cream base:**
   - In a saucepan, combine the heavy cream, whole milk, half of the sugar, and pinch of salt. Heat over medium heat, stirring occasionally, until the mixture is hot and just begins to bubble around the edges. Do not let it boil.
2. **Temper the eggs:**
   - In a separate bowl, whisk the egg yolks until smooth. Gradually whisk in about half of the hot cream mixture into the egg yolks to temper them.
3. **Combine and cook:**
   - Pour the tempered egg mixture back into the saucepan with the remaining cream mixture. Cook over medium-low heat, stirring constantly with a wooden spoon or spatula, until the custard thickens slightly and coats the back of the spoon (about 170-175°F or 77-80°C). Do not let it boil.
4. **Add vanilla extract:**
   - Remove the saucepan from heat and stir in the vanilla extract.
5. **Chill the custard:**
   - Strain the custard through a fine-mesh sieve into a clean bowl to remove any bits of cooked egg.
6. **Cool and churn:**
   - Cover the bowl with plastic wrap, pressing it directly onto the surface of the custard to prevent a skin from forming. Chill in the refrigerator for at least 4 hours or overnight.
7. **Churn the ice cream:**
   - Once chilled, churn the S'mores custard in an ice cream maker according to the manufacturer's instructions until it reaches a soft-serve consistency.

8. **Add mix-ins:**
   - During the last few minutes of churning, add the mini marshmallows, crushed graham crackers, and chocolate chunks into the ice cream maker, allowing them to mix evenly throughout the ice cream.
9. **Final freezing:**
   - Transfer the churned S'mores Ice Cream to a freezer-safe container, press a piece of parchment paper or plastic wrap directly onto the surface, and freeze until firm (usually 4-6 hours).
10. **Serve:**
    - Serve the S'mores Ice Cream scooped into bowls or cones, enjoying the delicious combination of chocolate, marshmallows, and graham crackers in every bite.

Enjoy your homemade S'mores Ice Cream! This recipe makes about 1 quart. Adjust the amount of mix-ins according to your preference for the perfect balance of flavors and textures.

Key Lime Pie Ice Cream

Ingredients:

- 1 cup sweetened condensed milk
- 1/2 cup fresh key lime juice (about 10-12 key limes)
- 1 tablespoon grated key lime zest
- 2 cups heavy cream
- 1 cup whole milk
- 3/4 cup granulated sugar
- Pinch of salt
- 1 teaspoon vanilla extract
- 1 cup crushed graham crackers (for swirling into ice cream)

Instructions:

1. **Prepare the ice cream base:**
   - In a bowl, whisk together the sweetened condensed milk, key lime juice, and grated key lime zest. Set aside.
2. **Make the custard base:**
   - In a saucepan, combine the heavy cream, whole milk, half of the sugar, and pinch of salt. Heat over medium heat, stirring occasionally, until the mixture is hot and just begins to bubble around the edges. Do not let it boil.
3. **Temper the eggs:**
   - In a separate bowl, whisk the egg yolks until smooth. Gradually whisk in about half of the hot cream mixture into the egg yolks to temper them.
4. **Combine and cook:**
   - Pour the tempered egg mixture back into the saucepan with the remaining cream mixture. Cook over medium-low heat, stirring constantly with a wooden spoon or spatula, until the custard thickens slightly and coats the back of the spoon (about 170-175°F or 77-80°C). Do not let it boil.
5. **Add vanilla extract:**
   - Remove the saucepan from heat and stir in the vanilla extract.
6. **Chill the custard:**
   - Strain the custard through a fine-mesh sieve into a clean bowl to remove any bits of cooked egg.
   - Stir in the key lime mixture (sweetened condensed milk, key lime juice, and zest) until well combined.

- Cover the bowl with plastic wrap, pressing it directly onto the surface of the custard to prevent a skin from forming. Chill in the refrigerator for at least 4 hours or overnight.

7. **Churn the ice cream:**
    - Once chilled, churn the Key Lime Pie custard in an ice cream maker according to the manufacturer's instructions until it reaches a soft-serve consistency.
8. **Add graham cracker swirl:**
    - During the last few minutes of churning, add the crushed graham crackers into the ice cream maker, allowing them to swirl evenly throughout the ice cream.
9. **Final freezing:**
    - Transfer the churned Key Lime Pie Ice Cream to a freezer-safe container, press a piece of parchment paper or plastic wrap directly onto the surface, and freeze until firm (usually 4-6 hours).
10. **Serve:**
    - Serve the Key Lime Pie Ice Cream scooped into bowls or cones, enjoying the tangy lime flavor and graham cracker swirl.

Enjoy your homemade Key Lime Pie Ice Cream! This recipe makes about 1 quart. Adjust the sweetness or tanginess by varying the amount of key lime juice and zest to suit your taste preference.

Birthday Cake Ice Cream

Ingredients:

- 2 cups heavy cream
- 1 cup whole milk
- 3/4 cup granulated sugar
- Pinch of salt
- 1 teaspoon vanilla extract
- 1/2 cup rainbow sprinkles (plus extra for garnish)
- 1/2 cup yellow cake mix (dry)
- 1/2 cup crushed cake pieces (from yellow cake or vanilla cake)
- 4 large egg yolks

Instructions:

1. **Prepare the ice cream base:**
   - In a saucepan, combine the heavy cream, whole milk, half of the sugar, and pinch of salt. Heat over medium heat, stirring occasionally, until the mixture is hot and just begins to bubble around the edges. Do not let it boil.
2. **Temper the eggs:**
   - In a separate bowl, whisk the egg yolks until smooth. Gradually whisk in about half of the hot cream mixture into the egg yolks to temper them.
3. **Combine and cook:**
   - Pour the tempered egg mixture back into the saucepan with the remaining cream mixture. Cook over medium-low heat, stirring constantly with a wooden spoon or spatula, until the custard thickens slightly and coats the back of the spoon (about 170-175°F or 77-80°C). Do not let it boil.
4. **Add vanilla extract and cake mix:**
   - Remove the saucepan from heat and stir in the vanilla extract.
   - Whisk in the dry yellow cake mix until fully incorporated.
5. **Chill the custard:**
   - Strain the custard through a fine-mesh sieve into a clean bowl to remove any bits of cooked egg.
   - Stir in the rainbow sprinkles and crushed cake pieces until evenly distributed.
   - Cover the bowl with plastic wrap, pressing it directly onto the surface of the custard to prevent a skin from forming. Chill in the refrigerator for at least 4 hours or overnight.

6. **Churn the ice cream:**
   - Once chilled, churn the Birthday Cake custard in an ice cream maker according to the manufacturer's instructions until it reaches a soft-serve consistency.
7. **Final freezing:**
   - Transfer the churned Birthday Cake Ice Cream to a freezer-safe container, press a piece of parchment paper or plastic wrap directly onto the surface, and freeze until firm (usually 4-6 hours).
8. **Serve:**
   - Serve the Birthday Cake Ice Cream scooped into bowls or cones, garnished with extra rainbow sprinkles if desired.

Enjoy your homemade Birthday Cake Ice Cream! This recipe makes about 1 quart. Adjust the amount of sprinkles and cake pieces according to your preference for a festive and celebratory treat.

Banana Pudding Ice Cream

Ingredients:

- 2 cups heavy cream
- 1 cup whole milk
- 3/4 cup granulated sugar
- Pinch of salt
- 1 teaspoon vanilla extract
- 3 ripe bananas, mashed
- 1/2 cup vanilla pudding mix (dry)
- 4 large egg yolks

Instructions:

1. **Prepare the ice cream base:**
    - In a saucepan, combine the heavy cream, whole milk, half of the sugar, and pinch of salt. Heat over medium heat, stirring occasionally, until the mixture is hot and just begins to bubble around the edges. Do not let it boil.
2. **Temper the eggs:**
    - In a separate bowl, whisk the egg yolks until smooth. Gradually whisk in about half of the hot cream mixture into the egg yolks to temper them.
3. **Combine and cook:**
    - Pour the tempered egg mixture back into the saucepan with the remaining cream mixture. Cook over medium-low heat, stirring constantly with a wooden spoon or spatula, until the custard thickens slightly and coats the back of the spoon (about 170-175°F or 77-80°C). Do not let it boil.
4. **Add vanilla extract, bananas, and pudding mix:**
    - Remove the saucepan from heat and stir in the vanilla extract.
    - Stir in the mashed bananas and vanilla pudding mix (dry) until fully incorporated.
5. **Chill the custard:**
    - Strain the custard through a fine-mesh sieve into a clean bowl to remove any bits of cooked egg.
    - Cover the bowl with plastic wrap, pressing it directly onto the surface of the custard to prevent a skin from forming. Chill in the refrigerator for at least 4 hours or overnight.
6. **Churn the ice cream:**

- Once chilled, churn the Banana Pudding custard in an ice cream maker according to the manufacturer's instructions until it reaches a soft-serve consistency.

7. **Final freezing:**
    - Transfer the churned Banana Pudding Ice Cream to a freezer-safe container, press a piece of parchment paper or plastic wrap directly onto the surface, and freeze until firm (usually 4-6 hours).
8. **Serve:**
    - Serve the Banana Pudding Ice Cream scooped into bowls or cones, enjoying the creamy banana and vanilla flavors.

Enjoy your homemade Banana Pudding Ice Cream! This recipe makes about 1 quart. Adjust the sweetness by varying the amount of sugar or adding more bananas according to your taste preference for a delightful frozen treat.

Caramel Swirl Ice Cream

Ingredients:

- 2 cups heavy cream
- 1 cup whole milk
- 3/4 cup granulated sugar
- Pinch of salt
- 1 teaspoon vanilla extract
- 1 cup caramel sauce (homemade or store-bought)

Instructions:

1. **Prepare the ice cream base:**
    - In a saucepan, combine the heavy cream, whole milk, half of the sugar, and pinch of salt. Heat over medium heat, stirring occasionally, until the mixture is hot and just begins to bubble around the edges. Do not let it boil.
2. **Temper the eggs:**
    - In a separate bowl, whisk the egg yolks until smooth. Gradually whisk in about half of the hot cream mixture into the egg yolks to temper them.
3. **Combine and cook:**
    - Pour the tempered egg mixture back into the saucepan with the remaining cream mixture. Cook over medium-low heat, stirring constantly with a wooden spoon or spatula, until the custard thickens slightly and coats the back of the spoon (about 170-175°F or 77-80°C). Do not let it boil.
4. **Add vanilla extract:**
    - Remove the saucepan from heat and stir in the vanilla extract.
5. **Chill the custard:**
    - Strain the custard through a fine-mesh sieve into a clean bowl to remove any bits of cooked egg.
    - Cover the bowl with plastic wrap, pressing it directly onto the surface of the custard to prevent a skin from forming. Chill in the refrigerator for at least 4 hours or overnight.
6. **Churn the ice cream:**
    - Once chilled, churn the Vanilla custard in an ice cream maker according to the manufacturer's instructions until it reaches a soft-serve consistency.
7. **Layer with caramel sauce:**
    - Transfer a layer of churned ice cream into a freezer-safe container. Drizzle some caramel sauce over the ice cream.

- Repeat layering ice cream and caramel sauce, swirling gently with a spoon or spatula to create ribbons of caramel throughout the ice cream.
8. **Final freezing:**
    - Press a piece of parchment paper or plastic wrap directly onto the surface of the ice cream to prevent ice crystals from forming. Freeze until firm (usually 4-6 hours).
9. **Serve:**
    - Serve the Caramel Swirl Ice Cream scooped into bowls or cones, enjoying the creamy vanilla base with decadent swirls of caramel sauce.

Enjoy your homemade Caramel Swirl Ice Cream! Adjust the amount of caramel sauce according to your preference for a richer or lighter caramel flavor.

Mocha Almond Fudge Ice Cream

Ingredients:

- 2 cups heavy cream
- 1 cup whole milk
- 3/4 cup granulated sugar
- Pinch of salt
- 1 teaspoon vanilla extract
- 2 tablespoons instant coffee or espresso powder
- 1/2 cup chocolate fudge sauce or hot fudge sauce
- 1/2 cup sliced almonds, toasted
- 4 large egg yolks

Instructions:

1. **Prepare the ice cream base:**
   - In a saucepan, combine the heavy cream, whole milk, half of the sugar, instant coffee or espresso powder, and pinch of salt. Heat over medium heat, stirring occasionally, until the mixture is hot and just begins to bubble around the edges. Do not let it boil.
2. **Temper the eggs:**
   - In a separate bowl, whisk the egg yolks until smooth. Gradually whisk in about half of the hot cream mixture into the egg yolks to temper them.
3. **Combine and cook:**
   - Pour the tempered egg mixture back into the saucepan with the remaining cream mixture. Cook over medium-low heat, stirring constantly with a wooden spoon or spatula, until the custard thickens slightly and coats the back of the spoon (about 170-175°F or 77-80°C). Do not let it boil.
4. **Add vanilla extract:**
   - Remove the saucepan from heat and stir in the vanilla extract.
5. **Chill the custard:**
   - Strain the custard through a fine-mesh sieve into a clean bowl to remove any bits of cooked egg.
   - Cover the bowl with plastic wrap, pressing it directly onto the surface of the custard to prevent a skin from forming. Chill in the refrigerator for at least 4 hours or overnight.
6. **Churn the ice cream:**
   - Once chilled, churn the Mocha custard in an ice cream maker according to the manufacturer's instructions until it reaches a soft-serve consistency.

7. **Add fudge sauce and almonds:**
    - During the last few minutes of churning, add the chocolate fudge sauce and toasted sliced almonds into the ice cream maker, allowing them to mix evenly throughout the ice cream.
8. **Final freezing:**
    - Transfer the churned Mocha Almond Fudge Ice Cream to a freezer-safe container. Press a piece of parchment paper or plastic wrap directly onto the surface of the ice cream to prevent ice crystals from forming.
9. **Serve:**
    - Freeze the ice cream until firm (usually 4-6 hours). Serve the Mocha Almond Fudge Ice Cream scooped into bowls or cones, enjoying the rich coffee and chocolate flavors with crunchy almonds and swirls of fudge.

Enjoy your homemade Mocha Almond Fudge Ice Cream! This recipe makes about 1 quart. Adjust the intensity of coffee flavor and sweetness by adjusting the amount of instant coffee/espresso and sugar to suit your taste preferences.

Coconut Ice Cream

Ingredients:

- 2 cups heavy cream
- 1 cup coconut milk (full-fat)
- 3/4 cup granulated sugar
- Pinch of salt
- 1 teaspoon vanilla extract
- 1 cup sweetened shredded coconut (optional, for texture)

Instructions:

1. **Prepare the ice cream base:**
    - In a saucepan, combine the heavy cream, coconut milk, half of the sugar, and pinch of salt. Heat over medium heat, stirring occasionally, until the mixture is hot and just begins to bubble around the edges. Do not let it boil.
2. **Combine and dissolve:**
    - Stir until the sugar is completely dissolved.
3. **Add vanilla extract:**
    - Remove the saucepan from heat and stir in the vanilla extract.
4. **Chill the mixture:**
    - Transfer the mixture to a bowl and let it cool to room temperature.
5. **Churn the ice cream:**
    - Once cooled, cover the bowl with plastic wrap and refrigerate for at least 4 hours or overnight until thoroughly chilled.
6. **Churn the ice cream:**
    - Churn the chilled coconut mixture in an ice cream maker according to the manufacturer's instructions until it reaches a soft-serve consistency.
7. **Add sweetened shredded coconut (optional):**
    - If desired, add the sweetened shredded coconut during the last few minutes of churning, allowing it to mix evenly throughout the ice cream.
8. **Final freezing:**
    - Transfer the churned Coconut Ice Cream to a freezer-safe container. Press a piece of parchment paper or plastic wrap directly onto the surface of the ice cream to prevent ice crystals from forming.
9. **Serve:**
    - Freeze the ice cream until firm (usually 4-6 hours). Serve the Coconut Ice Cream scooped into bowls or cones, enjoying the creamy coconut flavor.

Enjoy your homemade Coconut Ice Cream! This recipe makes about 1 quart. Adjust the sweetness by varying the amount of sugar to suit your taste preference, and feel free to add more shredded coconut for extra texture and coconut flavor.

Red Velvet Ice Cream

Ingredients:

- 2 cups heavy cream
- 1 cup whole milk
- 3/4 cup granulated sugar
- Pinch of salt
- 1 teaspoon vanilla extract
- 2 tablespoons cocoa powder
- 1 tablespoon red food coloring (gel or liquid)
- 1/2 cup cream cheese, softened
- 1/2 cup buttermilk
- 1 teaspoon vinegar
- 4 large egg yolks

Instructions:

1. **Prepare the ice cream base:**
   - In a saucepan, combine the heavy cream, whole milk, half of the sugar, cocoa powder, and pinch of salt. Heat over medium heat, stirring occasionally, until the mixture is hot and just begins to bubble around the edges. Do not let it boil.
2. **Temper the eggs:**
   - In a separate bowl, whisk the egg yolks until smooth. Gradually whisk in about half of the hot cream mixture into the egg yolks to temper them.
3. **Combine and cook:**
   - Pour the tempered egg mixture back into the saucepan with the remaining cream mixture. Cook over medium-low heat, stirring constantly with a wooden spoon or spatula, until the custard thickens slightly and coats the back of the spoon (about 170-175°F or 77-80°C). Do not let it boil.
4. **Add vanilla extract and red food coloring:**
   - Remove the saucepan from heat and stir in the vanilla extract and red food coloring until well combined.
5. **Prepare the red velvet mixture:**
   - In a separate bowl, whisk together the softened cream cheese, remaining sugar, buttermilk, and vinegar until smooth.
6. **Combine the mixtures:**
   - Gradually whisk the red velvet mixture into the custard until fully incorporated.

7. **Chill the custard:**
   - Strain the custard through a fine-mesh sieve into a clean bowl to remove any bits of cooked egg.
   - Cover the bowl with plastic wrap, pressing it directly onto the surface of the custard to prevent a skin from forming. Chill in the refrigerator for at least 4 hours or overnight.
8. **Churn the ice cream:**
   - Once chilled, churn the Red Velvet custard in an ice cream maker according to the manufacturer's instructions until it reaches a soft-serve consistency.
9. **Final freezing:**
   - Transfer the churned Red Velvet Ice Cream to a freezer-safe container. Press a piece of parchment paper or plastic wrap directly onto the surface of the ice cream to prevent ice crystals from forming.
10. **Serve:**
    - Freeze the ice cream until firm (usually 4-6 hours). Serve the Red Velvet Ice Cream scooped into bowls or cones, enjoying the rich, chocolatey, and tangy flavors reminiscent of red velvet cake.

Enjoy your homemade Red Velvet Ice Cream! This recipe makes about 1 quart. Adjust the intensity of red food coloring and sweetness according to your preference for a deliciously unique ice cream experience.

Lemon Sorbet

Ingredients:

- 1 cup water
- 1 cup granulated sugar
- 1 cup fresh lemon juice (from about 5-6 lemons)
- 1 tablespoon lemon zest (optional, for extra lemon flavor)

Instructions:

1. **Make the simple syrup:**
    - In a small saucepan, combine water and granulated sugar. Heat over medium heat, stirring occasionally, until the sugar completely dissolves and the mixture just begins to simmer. Remove from heat and let cool to room temperature.
2. **Prepare the lemon mixture:**
    - In a bowl, combine the fresh lemon juice and lemon zest (if using).
3. **Combine and chill:**
    - Stir the cooled simple syrup into the lemon juice mixture until well combined. Cover the bowl with plastic wrap and refrigerate for at least 1-2 hours to chill thoroughly.
4. **Churn the sorbet:**
    - Once chilled, pour the lemon mixture into an ice cream maker and churn according to the manufacturer's instructions until it reaches a slushy, sorbet-like consistency.
5. **Final freezing:**
    - Transfer the churned Lemon Sorbet into a freezer-safe container. Press a piece of parchment paper or plastic wrap directly onto the surface of the sorbet to prevent ice crystals from forming.
6. **Serve:**
    - Freeze the Lemon Sorbet until firm (usually 3-4 hours). Serve scooped into bowls or cones, garnished with fresh mint leaves or a slice of lemon for a refreshing finish.

Enjoy your homemade Lemon Sorbet! This recipe yields approximately 1 quart of sorbet. Adjust the sweetness and tartness by varying the amount of sugar and lemon juice according to your taste preferences.

Orange Sherbet

Ingredients:

- 2 cups fresh orange juice (about 4-5 large oranges)
- 1 cup granulated sugar
- 1 cup milk (whole milk or reduced-fat milk)
- 1 teaspoon vanilla extract
- Pinch of salt

Instructions:

1. **Prepare the Orange Mixture:**
    - In a medium bowl, whisk together the fresh orange juice and granulated sugar until the sugar is completely dissolved.
2. **Combine Ingredients:**
    - Stir in the milk, vanilla extract, and a pinch of salt until everything is well combined. Make sure the mixture is smooth.
3. **Chill the Mixture:**
    - Cover the bowl and refrigerate the mixture for at least 2 hours, or until it is thoroughly chilled. This step helps the flavors to meld together.
4. **Churn in Ice Cream Maker:**
    - Once chilled, pour the sherbet mixture into your ice cream maker and churn according to the manufacturer's instructions, typically about 20-30 minutes, or until it reaches a soft-serve consistency.
5. **Transfer and Freeze:**
    - Transfer the sherbet to an airtight container and freeze for at least 4 hours or until firm before serving.
6. **Serve:**
    - Scoop the orange sherbet into bowls or cones and enjoy!

This recipe yields a creamy and tangy orange sherbet that's perfect for a refreshing treat on a hot day. Enjoy making and savoring it!

Peach Ice Cream

Ingredients:

- 2 cups ripe peaches, peeled and chopped (about 4-5 medium peaches)
- 1 tablespoon lemon juice
- 3/4 cup granulated sugar
- 1 cup whole milk
- 2 cups heavy cream
- 1 teaspoon vanilla extract

Instructions:

1. **Prepare the Peaches:**
    - In a bowl, toss the chopped peaches with lemon juice and 1/4 cup of the sugar. Let them sit for about 15-20 minutes until they release their juices.
2. **Blend the Peaches:**
    - Transfer the peaches and their juices into a blender or food processor. Pulse until the mixture is pureed but still slightly chunky. You can adjust the texture to your preference.
3. **Combine Ingredients:**
    - In a separate bowl, whisk together the remaining 1/2 cup sugar, whole milk, heavy cream, and vanilla extract until the sugar is dissolved.
4. **Mix and Chill:**
    - Stir the peach puree into the milk and cream mixture until well combined. Cover the bowl and refrigerate for at least 2 hours, or until thoroughly chilled.
5. **Churn in Ice Cream Maker:**
    - Once chilled, pour the peach ice cream base into your ice cream maker and churn according to the manufacturer's instructions, typically about 20-30 minutes, or until it reaches a soft-serve consistency.
6. **Transfer and Freeze:**
    - Transfer the churned peach ice cream into a freezer-safe container. Press a piece of parchment paper or plastic wrap directly onto the surface of the ice cream to prevent ice crystals from forming. Freeze for at least 4 hours, or until firm.
7. **Serve:**
    - Scoop the peach ice cream into bowls or cones and enjoy the fresh, fruity flavor!

This recipe yields a creamy peach ice cream with real fruit flavor that's perfect for enjoying during peach season or any time you crave a taste of summer.

Blueberry Cheesecake Ice Cream

Ingredients:

For the Blueberry Sauce:

- 1 cup fresh or frozen blueberries
- 1/4 cup granulated sugar
- 1 tablespoon lemon juice

For the Cheesecake Ice Cream Base:

- 8 oz (225g) cream cheese, softened
- 1 cup granulated sugar
- 1 cup whole milk
- 2 cups heavy cream
- 1 teaspoon vanilla extract
- 1 cup graham crackers, crushed (optional, for added texture)

Instructions:

1. **Prepare the Blueberry Sauce:**
   - In a small saucepan, combine the blueberries, sugar, and lemon juice. Cook over medium heat, stirring occasionally, until the blueberries release their juices and the mixture thickens slightly, about 5-7 minutes. Remove from heat and let it cool completely.
2. **Make the Cheesecake Ice Cream Base:**
   - In a large bowl, beat the softened cream cheese until smooth. Add the granulated sugar and mix until well combined and creamy.
3. **Combine Ingredients:**
   - Stir in the whole milk, heavy cream, and vanilla extract until the mixture is smooth and all ingredients are incorporated. If using, fold in the crushed graham crackers for added texture.
4. **Chill the Mixture:**
   - Cover the bowl and refrigerate the cheesecake ice cream base for at least 2 hours, or until thoroughly chilled.
5. **Churn in Ice Cream Maker:**
   - Once chilled, pour the cheesecake ice cream base into your ice cream maker and churn according to the manufacturer's instructions, typically about 20-30 minutes, or until it reaches a soft-serve consistency.
6. **Swirl in the Blueberry Sauce:**

- Transfer about half of the churned ice cream into a freezer-safe container. Spoon half of the cooled blueberry sauce over the ice cream. Repeat with the remaining ice cream and blueberry sauce, creating swirls as you layer.

7. **Freeze:**
    - Use a knife or spoon handle to gently swirl the blueberry sauce through the ice cream, creating a marbled effect. Cover the container with a lid or plastic wrap and freeze for at least 4 hours, or until firm.
8. **Serve:**
    - Scoop the blueberry cheesecake ice cream into bowls or cones and enjoy the creamy, tangy flavors!

This recipe combines the richness of cheesecake with the fruity sweetness of blueberries, creating a delicious homemade ice cream that's perfect for summer or any time you crave a decadent treat.

Apple Pie Ice Cream

Ingredients:

For the Apple Pie Filling:

- 2 cups apples, peeled and diced (about 2 medium apples)
- 2 tablespoons unsalted butter
- 1/4 cup brown sugar
- 1 teaspoon ground cinnamon
- 1/4 teaspoon ground nutmeg
- Pinch of salt

For the Ice Cream Base:

- 1 cup whole milk
- 2 cups heavy cream
- 3/4 cup granulated sugar
- 1 teaspoon vanilla extract
- 1/2 cup graham crackers, crushed (optional, for pie crust texture)

Instructions:

1. **Prepare the Apple Pie Filling:**
    - In a large skillet or saucepan, melt the butter over medium heat. Add the diced apples, brown sugar, cinnamon, nutmeg, and salt. Cook, stirring occasionally, until the apples are tender and caramelized, about 8-10 minutes. Remove from heat and let it cool completely.
2. **Make the Ice Cream Base:**
    - In a large bowl, whisk together the whole milk, heavy cream, granulated sugar, and vanilla extract until the sugar is dissolved and the mixture is smooth. If using, fold in the crushed graham crackers for added pie crust texture.
3. **Combine the Ingredients:**
    - Stir the cooled apple pie filling into the ice cream base until well combined. Make sure the apples are evenly distributed throughout the mixture.
4. **Chill the Mixture:**
    - Cover the bowl and refrigerate the apple pie ice cream base for at least 2 hours, or until thoroughly chilled.
5. **Churn in Ice Cream Maker:**

        - Once chilled, pour the apple pie ice cream base into your ice cream maker and churn according to the manufacturer's instructions, typically about 20-30 minutes, or until it reaches a soft-serve consistency.
6. **Freeze:**
        - Transfer the churned ice cream into a freezer-safe container. Cover with a lid or plastic wrap and freeze for at least 4 hours, or until firm.
7. **Serve:**
        - Scoop the apple pie ice cream into bowls or cones and enjoy the delightful flavors reminiscent of homemade apple pie!

This recipe captures the essence of apple pie with caramelized apples and warming spices, combined with a creamy ice cream base for a delightful dessert experience.

Snickerdoodle Ice Cream

Ingredients:

For the Snickerdoodle Cookie Crumbs:

- 1 cup all-purpose flour
- 1/2 teaspoon baking soda
- 1/4 teaspoon cream of tartar
- 1/4 teaspoon salt
- 1/2 cup unsalted butter, softened
- 1/2 cup granulated sugar
- 1/4 cup packed light brown sugar
- 1 large egg
- 1/2 teaspoon vanilla extract
- 1 tablespoon granulated sugar + 1 teaspoon ground cinnamon (for rolling cookies)

For the Ice Cream Base:

- 1 cup whole milk
- 2 cups heavy cream
- 3/4 cup granulated sugar
- 1 teaspoon vanilla extract
- 1 teaspoon ground cinnamon

Instructions:

1. **Make Snickerdoodle Cookie Crumbs:**
    - Preheat your oven to 350°F (175°C). Line a baking sheet with parchment paper.
    - In a medium bowl, whisk together the flour, baking soda, cream of tartar, and salt.
    - In a separate large bowl, beat together the softened butter, granulated sugar, and brown sugar until light and fluffy. Add the egg and vanilla extract, beating until well combined.
    - Gradually add the dry ingredients to the wet ingredients, mixing until just combined.
    - In a small bowl, mix together the remaining tablespoon of granulated sugar and teaspoon of ground cinnamon.

- Shape the dough into 1-inch balls, then roll each ball in the cinnamon-sugar mixture until coated.
    - Place the coated dough balls onto the prepared baking sheet, spacing them about 2 inches apart. Flatten each ball slightly with the bottom of a glass.
    - Bake for 10-12 minutes, or until the edges are set and just lightly golden. Remove from the oven and let the cookies cool completely on a wire rack. Once cooled, break the cookies into small crumbs. Set aside.
2. **Make the Ice Cream Base:**
    - In a large bowl, whisk together the whole milk, heavy cream, granulated sugar, vanilla extract, and ground cinnamon until the sugar is dissolved and the mixture is smooth.
3. **Assemble the Ice Cream:**
    - Stir the snickerdoodle cookie crumbs into the ice cream base until well combined.
4. **Chill the Mixture:**
    - Cover the bowl and refrigerate the snickerdoodle ice cream base for at least 2 hours, or until thoroughly chilled.
5. **Churn in Ice Cream Maker:**
    - Once chilled, pour the snickerdoodle ice cream base into your ice cream maker and churn according to the manufacturer's instructions, typically about 20-30 minutes, or until it reaches a soft-serve consistency.
6. **Freeze:**
    - Transfer the churned ice cream into a freezer-safe container. Cover with a lid or plastic wrap, pressing it directly onto the surface of the ice cream to prevent ice crystals from forming. Freeze for at least 4 hours, or until firm.
7. **Serve:**
    - Scoop the snickerdoodle ice cream into bowls or cones and enjoy the delightful cinnamon-sugar flavors in every bite!

This recipe captures the essence of snickerdoodle cookies in a creamy ice cream form, perfect for satisfying your sweet tooth with a nostalgic twist.

Maple Walnut Ice Cream

Ingredients:

- 1 cup pure maple syrup
- 1 cup walnuts, chopped
- 2 cups heavy cream
- 1 cup whole milk
- 3/4 cup granulated sugar
- 4 large egg yolks
- 1 teaspoon vanilla extract
- Pinch of salt

Instructions:

1. **Prepare the Maple Syrup and Walnuts:**
   - In a small saucepan, heat the maple syrup over medium heat until it starts to simmer. Remove from heat and stir in the chopped walnuts. Let the mixture cool to room temperature, then refrigerate until needed.
2. **Make the Ice Cream Base:**
   - In a medium saucepan, combine the heavy cream, whole milk, and half of the granulated sugar (about 6 tablespoons). Heat over medium heat until it just begins to simmer, stirring occasionally. Remove from heat.
3. **Whisk the Egg Yolks:**
   - In a separate bowl, whisk together the egg yolks and the remaining sugar (about 6 tablespoons) until pale and slightly thickened.
4. **Temper the Eggs:**
   - Gradually pour about half of the hot cream mixture into the bowl with the egg yolks, whisking constantly to temper the eggs and prevent them from scrambling.
5. **Combine and Cook:**
   - Pour the tempered egg mixture back into the saucepan with the remaining hot cream mixture. Cook over low heat, stirring constantly, until the custard thickens slightly and coats the back of a spoon (about 170-175°F or 77-80°C on an instant-read thermometer).
6. **Strain and Chill:**
   - Strain the custard through a fine-mesh sieve into a clean bowl. Stir in the vanilla extract and a pinch of salt. Place the bowl in an ice bath to cool the custard quickly, then cover and refrigerate until thoroughly chilled (at least 4 hours or overnight).

7. **Churn in Ice Cream Maker:**
   - Once chilled, pour the maple walnut mixture (including the maple syrup and walnuts) into your ice cream maker and churn according to the manufacturer's instructions, typically about 20-30 minutes, or until it reaches a soft-serve consistency.
8. **Freeze:**
   - Transfer the churned ice cream into a freezer-safe container. Cover with a lid or plastic wrap, pressing it directly onto the surface of the ice cream to prevent ice crystals from forming. Freeze for at least 4 hours, or until firm.
9. **Serve:**
   - Scoop the maple walnut ice cream into bowls or cones and enjoy the rich, nutty flavors with crunchy bites of walnuts in every spoonful!

This recipe captures the distinctive taste of maple syrup and the crunch of walnuts, making it a delightful treat for maple syrup lovers and ice cream aficionados alike.

Pumpkin Pie Ice Cream

Ingredients:

For the Pumpkin Puree:

- 1 cup canned pumpkin puree (not pumpkin pie filling)
- 1 teaspoon ground cinnamon
- 1/2 teaspoon ground ginger
- 1/4 teaspoon ground nutmeg
- 1/4 teaspoon ground cloves

For the Ice Cream Base:

- 2 cups heavy cream
- 1 cup whole milk
- 3/4 cup granulated sugar
- 4 large egg yolks
- 1 teaspoon vanilla extract
- 1/2 teaspoon ground cinnamon
- 1/4 teaspoon ground ginger
- 1/4 teaspoon ground nutmeg
- 1/4 teaspoon salt

Instructions:

1. **Prepare the Pumpkin Puree:**
    - In a small bowl, mix together the pumpkin puree, ground cinnamon, ground ginger, ground nutmeg, and ground cloves until well combined. Set aside.
2. **Make the Ice Cream Base:**
    - In a medium saucepan, combine the heavy cream, whole milk, and half of the granulated sugar (about 6 tablespoons). Heat over medium heat until it just begins to simmer, stirring occasionally. Remove from heat.
3. **Whisk the Egg Yolks:**
    - In a separate bowl, whisk together the egg yolks and the remaining sugar (about 6 tablespoons) until pale and slightly thickened.
4. **Temper the Eggs:**
    - Gradually pour about half of the hot cream mixture into the bowl with the egg yolks, whisking constantly to temper the eggs and prevent them from scrambling.
5. **Combine and Cook:**

- Pour the tempered egg mixture back into the saucepan with the remaining hot cream mixture. Cook over low heat, stirring constantly, until the custard thickens slightly and coats the back of a spoon (about 170-175°F or 77-80°C on an instant-read thermometer).

6. **Combine with Pumpkin Puree:**
   - Remove the custard from heat and stir in the vanilla extract, ground cinnamon, ground ginger, ground nutmeg, and salt. Whisk in the prepared pumpkin puree until smooth and well combined.

7. **Chill the Mixture:**
   - Strain the custard through a fine-mesh sieve into a clean bowl to remove any lumps. Place the bowl in an ice bath to cool the custard quickly, then cover and refrigerate until thoroughly chilled (at least 4 hours or overnight).

8. **Churn in Ice Cream Maker:**
   - Once chilled, pour the pumpkin pie ice cream base into your ice cream maker and churn according to the manufacturer's instructions, typically about 20-30 minutes, or until it reaches a soft-serve consistency.

9. **Freeze:**
   - Transfer the churned ice cream into a freezer-safe container. Cover with a lid or plastic wrap, pressing it directly onto the surface of the ice cream to prevent ice crystals from forming. Freeze for at least 4 hours, or until firm.

10. **Serve:**
    - Scoop the pumpkin pie ice cream into bowls or cones and enjoy the creamy, spiced flavors reminiscent of pumpkin pie!

This recipe captures the essence of pumpkin pie in a creamy ice cream form, perfect for enjoying during the fall season or whenever you're craving a taste of pumpkin pie with a twist.

Eggnog Ice Cream

Ingredients:

- 2 cups heavy cream
- 1 cup whole milk
- 3/4 cup granulated sugar
- 4 large egg yolks
- 1/2 teaspoon ground nutmeg
- 1/4 teaspoon ground cinnamon
- 1/4 teaspoon vanilla extract
- Pinch of salt
- 1/4 cup dark rum or bourbon (optional, for adults)

Instructions:

1. **Prepare the Base:**
   - In a medium saucepan, combine the heavy cream, whole milk, nutmeg, cinnamon, vanilla extract, and salt. Heat over medium heat until it just begins to simmer, stirring occasionally. Remove from heat.
2. **Whisk the Egg Yolks:**
   - In a separate bowl, whisk together the egg yolks and granulated sugar until pale and slightly thickened.
3. **Temper the Eggs:**
   - Gradually pour about half of the hot cream mixture into the bowl with the egg yolks, whisking constantly to temper the eggs and prevent them from scrambling.
4. **Combine and Cook:**
   - Pour the tempered egg mixture back into the saucepan with the remaining hot cream mixture. Cook over low heat, stirring constantly, until the custard thickens slightly and coats the back of a spoon (about 170-175°F or 77-80°C on an instant-read thermometer).
5. **Optional: Add Rum or Bourbon (Adults Only):**
   - If using, stir in the dark rum or bourbon into the custard mixture. Adjust the amount to your taste preference.
6. **Chill the Mixture:**
   - Strain the custard through a fine-mesh sieve into a clean bowl to remove any lumps and allow the flavors to meld. Place the bowl in an ice bath to cool the custard quickly, then cover and refrigerate until thoroughly chilled (at least 4 hours or overnight).

7. **Churn in Ice Cream Maker:**
   - Once chilled, pour the eggnog ice cream base into your ice cream maker and churn according to the manufacturer's instructions, typically about 20-30 minutes, or until it reaches a soft-serve consistency.
8. **Freeze:**
   - Transfer the churned eggnog ice cream into a freezer-safe container. Cover with a lid or plastic wrap, pressing it directly onto the surface of the ice cream to prevent ice crystals from forming. Freeze for at least 4 hours, or until firm.
9. **Serve:**
   - Scoop the eggnog ice cream into bowls or cones and enjoy the creamy, spiced flavors reminiscent of the holiday drink!

This recipe captures the essence of eggnog in a delightful frozen dessert, perfect for holiday gatherings or any time you crave the flavors of eggnog in a new form. Adjust the spices and optional alcohol to suit your taste preferences.

Rum Raisin Ice Cream

Ingredients:

- 1 cup raisins
- 1/4 cup dark rum
- 2 cups heavy cream
- 1 cup whole milk
- 3/4 cup granulated sugar
- 4 large egg yolks
- 1 teaspoon vanilla extract
- Pinch of salt

Instructions:

1. **Prepare the Rum Raisins:**
    - In a small saucepan, heat the rum over low heat until it starts to simmer. Remove from heat and add the raisins. Let them soak in the rum for at least 30 minutes, stirring occasionally, until plumped and infused with rum flavor. Drain the raisins, reserving the rum for later use.
2. **Make the Ice Cream Base:**
    - In a medium saucepan, combine the heavy cream, whole milk, and half of the granulated sugar (about 6 tablespoons). Heat over medium heat until it just begins to simmer, stirring occasionally. Remove from heat.
3. **Whisk the Egg Yolks:**
    - In a separate bowl, whisk together the egg yolks and the remaining sugar (about 6 tablespoons) until pale and slightly thickened.
4. **Temper the Eggs:**
    - Gradually pour about half of the hot cream mixture into the bowl with the egg yolks, whisking constantly to temper the eggs and prevent them from scrambling.
5. **Combine and Cook:**
    - Pour the tempered egg mixture back into the saucepan with the remaining hot cream mixture. Cook over low heat, stirring constantly, until the custard thickens slightly and coats the back of a spoon (about 170-175°F or 77-80°C on an instant-read thermometer).
6. **Add Vanilla and Rum:**
    - Remove the custard from heat and stir in the vanilla extract and reserved rum (from soaking the raisins). Stir until well combined.
7. **Chill the Mixture:**

- Strain the custard through a fine-mesh sieve into a clean bowl to remove any lumps. Place the bowl in an ice bath to cool the custard quickly, then cover and refrigerate until thoroughly chilled (at least 4 hours or overnight).

8. **Churn in Ice Cream Maker:**
    - Once chilled, pour the rum-infused custard base into your ice cream maker and churn according to the manufacturer's instructions, typically about 20-30 minutes, or until it reaches a soft-serve consistency.
9. **Add Rum Raisins:**
    - During the last 5 minutes of churning, add the plumped rum-soaked raisins into the ice cream maker, allowing them to mix evenly throughout the ice cream.
10. **Freeze:**
    - Transfer the churned rum raisin ice cream into a freezer-safe container. Cover with a lid or plastic wrap, pressing it directly onto the surface of the ice cream to prevent ice crystals from forming. Freeze for at least 4 hours, or until firm.
11. **Serve:**
    - Scoop the creamy rum raisin ice cream into bowls or cones and enjoy the delightful combination of rum-infused custard and plump, flavorful raisins!

This recipe yields a rich and indulgent rum raisin ice cream that's perfect for enjoying as a dessert on its own or paired with desserts like warm apple pie or brownies. Adjust the rum quantity to your preference for a more pronounced or subtle boozy flavor.

Toffee Crunch Ice Cream

Ingredients:

- 1 cup toffee pieces or crushed toffee candy (such as Heath bars)
- 2 cups heavy cream
- 1 cup whole milk
- 3/4 cup granulated sugar
- 4 large egg yolks
- 1 teaspoon vanilla extract
- Pinch of salt

Instructions:

1. **Prepare the Toffee Pieces:**
    - If you're using toffee candy bars, crush them into small pieces. You can do this by placing the bars in a plastic bag and using a rolling pin to crush them. Set aside.
2. **Make the Ice Cream Base:**
    - In a medium saucepan, combine the heavy cream, whole milk, and half of the granulated sugar (about 6 tablespoons). Heat over medium heat until it just begins to simmer, stirring occasionally. Remove from heat.
3. **Whisk the Egg Yolks:**
    - In a separate bowl, whisk together the egg yolks and the remaining sugar (about 6 tablespoons) until pale and slightly thickened.
4. **Temper the Eggs:**
    - Gradually pour about half of the hot cream mixture into the bowl with the egg yolks, whisking constantly to temper the eggs and prevent them from scrambling.
5. **Combine and Cook:**
    - Pour the tempered egg mixture back into the saucepan with the remaining hot cream mixture. Cook over low heat, stirring constantly, until the custard thickens slightly and coats the back of a spoon (about 170-175°F or 77-80°C on an instant-read thermometer).
6. **Add Vanilla and Chill:**
    - Remove the custard from heat and stir in the vanilla extract and a pinch of salt. Stir until well combined. Strain the custard through a fine-mesh sieve into a clean bowl to remove any lumps. Place the bowl in an ice bath to cool the custard quickly, then cover and refrigerate until thoroughly chilled (at least 4 hours or overnight).

7. **Churn in Ice Cream Maker:**
   - Once chilled, pour the toffee-infused custard base into your ice cream maker and churn according to the manufacturer's instructions, typically about 20-30 minutes, or until it reaches a soft-serve consistency.
8. **Add Toffee Pieces:**
   - During the last 5 minutes of churning, add the crushed toffee pieces into the ice cream maker, allowing them to mix evenly throughout the ice cream.
9. **Freeze:**
   - Transfer the churned toffee crunch ice cream into a freezer-safe container. Cover with a lid or plastic wrap, pressing it directly onto the surface of the ice cream to prevent ice crystals from forming. Freeze for at least 4 hours, or until firm.
10. **Serve:**
    - Scoop the creamy toffee crunch ice cream into bowls or cones and enjoy the delightful combination of creamy custard and crunchy toffee pieces!

This recipe yields a rich and crunchy toffee crunch ice cream that's perfect for satisfying your sweet tooth. It's a crowd-pleasing dessert that can be enjoyed on its own or paired with your favorite baked goods.

Honeycomb Ice Cream

Ingredients:

For the Honeycomb Candy:

- 1 cup granulated sugar
- 1/4 cup honey
- 1/4 cup water
- 1 tablespoon baking soda

For the Ice Cream Base:

- 2 cups heavy cream
- 1 cup whole milk
- 3/4 cup granulated sugar
- 4 large egg yolks
- 1 teaspoon vanilla extract
- Pinch of salt

Instructions:

1. **Prepare the Honeycomb Candy:**
    - Line a baking sheet with parchment paper or a silicone mat.
    - In a medium saucepan, combine the granulated sugar, honey, and water. Stir over medium heat until the sugar dissolves.
    - Once the mixture starts to boil, stop stirring and let it cook until it reaches 300°F (150°C) on a candy thermometer, which is the hard crack stage.
    - Quickly whisk in the baking soda until it foams up, then pour the mixture onto the prepared baking sheet. Allow it to cool and harden completely. Once cooled, break or chop the honeycomb into small pieces. Set aside.
2. **Make the Ice Cream Base:**
    - In a medium saucepan, combine the heavy cream, whole milk, and half of the granulated sugar (about 6 tablespoons). Heat over medium heat until it just begins to simmer, stirring occasionally. Remove from heat.
3. **Whisk the Egg Yolks:**
    - In a separate bowl, whisk together the egg yolks and the remaining sugar (about 6 tablespoons) until pale and slightly thickened.
4. **Temper the Eggs:**

- Gradually pour about half of the hot cream mixture into the bowl with the egg yolks, whisking constantly to temper the eggs and prevent them from scrambling.

5. **Combine and Cook:**
   - Pour the tempered egg mixture back into the saucepan with the remaining hot cream mixture. Cook over low heat, stirring constantly, until the custard thickens slightly and coats the back of a spoon (about 170-175°F or 77-80°C on an instant-read thermometer).

6. **Add Vanilla and Chill:**
   - Remove the custard from heat and stir in the vanilla extract and a pinch of salt. Stir until well combined. Strain the custard through a fine-mesh sieve into a clean bowl to remove any lumps. Place the bowl in an ice bath to cool the custard quickly, then cover and refrigerate until thoroughly chilled (at least 4 hours or overnight).

7. **Churn in Ice Cream Maker:**
   - Once chilled, pour the honeycomb-infused custard base into your ice cream maker and churn according to the manufacturer's instructions, typically about 20-30 minutes, or until it reaches a soft-serve consistency.

8. **Add Honeycomb Pieces:**
   - During the last 5 minutes of churning, add the chopped honeycomb pieces into the ice cream maker, allowing them to mix evenly throughout the ice cream.

9. **Freeze:**
   - Transfer the churned honeycomb ice cream into a freezer-safe container. Cover with a lid or plastic wrap, pressing it directly onto the surface of the ice cream to prevent ice crystals from forming. Freeze for at least 4 hours, or until firm.

10. **Serve:**
    - Scoop the creamy honeycomb ice cream into bowls or cones and enjoy the delightful combination of creamy custard and crunchy honeycomb pieces!

This recipe captures the essence of honeycomb in a creamy ice cream form, perfect for enjoying as a special treat. Adjust the amount of honeycomb pieces to your liking for more or less crunch in each bite.

Almond Joy Ice Cream

Ingredients:

- 1 cup shredded sweetened coconut
- 1/2 cup whole almonds, chopped
- 2 cups heavy cream
- 1 cup whole milk
- 3/4 cup granulated sugar
- 4 large egg yolks
- 1 teaspoon vanilla extract
- Pinch of salt
- 1/2 cup semi-sweet chocolate chips or chopped chocolate

Instructions:

1. **Toast the Coconut and Almonds:**
   - Preheat your oven to 325°F (160°C). Spread the shredded coconut and chopped almonds on a baking sheet in an even layer.
   - Toast in the preheated oven for about 5-7 minutes, stirring occasionally, until the coconut turns golden brown and fragrant. Watch closely to prevent burning. Remove from the oven and let cool.
2. **Make the Ice Cream Base:**
   - In a medium saucepan, combine the heavy cream, whole milk, and half of the granulated sugar (about 6 tablespoons). Heat over medium heat until it just begins to simmer, stirring occasionally. Remove from heat.
3. **Whisk the Egg Yolks:**
   - In a separate bowl, whisk together the egg yolks and the remaining sugar (about 6 tablespoons) until pale and slightly thickened.
4. **Temper the Eggs:**
   - Gradually pour about half of the hot cream mixture into the bowl with the egg yolks, whisking constantly to temper the eggs and prevent them from scrambling.
5. **Combine and Cook:**
   - Pour the tempered egg mixture back into the saucepan with the remaining hot cream mixture. Cook over low heat, stirring constantly, until the custard thickens slightly and coats the back of a spoon (about 170-175°F or 77-80°C on an instant-read thermometer).
6. **Add Vanilla and Chill:**

- Remove the custard from heat and stir in the vanilla extract and a pinch of salt. Stir until well combined. Strain the custard through a fine-mesh sieve into a clean bowl to remove any lumps. Place the bowl in an ice bath to cool the custard quickly, then cover and refrigerate until thoroughly chilled (at least 4 hours or overnight).

7. **Churn in Ice Cream Maker:**
   - Once chilled, pour the almond joy-infused custard base into your ice cream maker and churn according to the manufacturer's instructions, typically about 20-30 minutes, or until it reaches a soft-serve consistency.

8. **Add Coconut, Almonds, and Chocolate:**
   - During the last 5 minutes of churning, add the toasted coconut, chopped almonds, and semi-sweet chocolate chips or chopped chocolate into the ice cream maker, allowing them to mix evenly throughout the ice cream.

9. **Freeze:**
   - Transfer the churned almond joy ice cream into a freezer-safe container. Cover with a lid or plastic wrap, pressing it directly onto the surface of the ice cream to prevent ice crystals from forming. Freeze for at least 4 hours, or until firm.

10. **Serve:**
    - Scoop the creamy almond joy ice cream into bowls or cones and enjoy the delightful combination of coconut, almonds, and chocolate flavors!

This recipe captures the essence of the beloved Almond Joy candy bar in a creamy ice cream form, perfect for satisfying your sweet tooth with a homemade twist. Adjust the ingredients to your liking for more or less crunch and chocolate in each bite.

Salted Caramel Pretzel Ice Cream

Ingredients:

For the Salted Caramel Sauce:

- 1 cup granulated sugar
- 6 tablespoons unsalted butter, cut into pieces
- 1/2 cup heavy cream
- 1 teaspoon sea salt (adjust to taste)

For the Ice Cream Base:

- 2 cups heavy cream
- 1 cup whole milk
- 3/4 cup granulated sugar
- 4 large egg yolks
- 1 teaspoon vanilla extract
- Pinch of salt
- 1 cup pretzels, coarsely chopped (salted or unsalted, depending on preference)

Instructions:

1. **Make the Salted Caramel Sauce:**
    - In a heavy-bottomed saucepan, heat the granulated sugar over medium heat, stirring constantly with a high heat resistant rubber spatula or wooden spoon. The sugar will begin to form clumps and eventually melt into a thick, amber-colored liquid as you continue to stir. Be careful not to burn it.
    - Once the sugar is completely melted, immediately add the butter. The caramel will bubble rapidly when you add the butter, so be cautious.
    - Stir the butter into the caramel until it is completely melted, about 2-3 minutes. If the butter separates, remove the pan from heat and whisk vigorously to combine it again.
    - Remove the pan from the heat and carefully pour in the heavy cream. The mixture will bubble again. Whisk until the cream is incorporated and the sauce is smooth.
2. Transfer the salted caramel sauce to a heatproof container and allow it to cool slightly. Stir in the sea salt to taste. Set aside until ready to use.

Cinnamon Roll Ice Cream

Ingredients:

For the Cinnamon Roll Swirl:

- 1/2 cup brown sugar, packed
- 2 tablespoons unsalted butter
- 1 teaspoon ground cinnamon

For the Ice Cream Base:

- 2 cups heavy cream
- 1 cup whole milk
- 3/4 cup granulated sugar
- 4 large egg yolks
- 1 teaspoon vanilla extract
- Pinch of salt

Instructions:

1. **Prepare the Cinnamon Roll Swirl:**
   - In a small saucepan over medium heat, melt the butter. Add the brown sugar and ground cinnamon, stirring until the sugar is dissolved and the mixture is smooth. Remove from heat and let cool to room temperature.
2. **Make the Ice Cream Base:**
   - In a medium saucepan, combine the heavy cream, whole milk, and half of the granulated sugar (about 6 tablespoons). Heat over medium heat until it just begins to simmer, stirring occasionally. Remove from heat.
3. **Whisk the Egg Yolks:**
   - In a separate bowl, whisk together the egg yolks and the remaining sugar (about 6 tablespoons) until pale and slightly thickened.
4. **Temper the Eggs:**
   - Gradually pour about half of the hot cream mixture into the bowl with the egg yolks, whisking constantly to temper the eggs and prevent them from scrambling.
5. **Combine and Cook:**
   - Pour the tempered egg mixture back into the saucepan with the remaining hot cream mixture. Cook over low heat, stirring constantly, until the custard thickens slightly and coats the back of a spoon (about 170-175°F or 77-80°C on an instant-read thermometer).

6. **Add Vanilla and Chill:**
   - Remove the custard from heat and stir in the vanilla extract and a pinch of salt. Stir until well combined. Strain the custard through a fine-mesh sieve into a clean bowl to remove any lumps. Place the bowl in an ice bath to cool the custard quickly, then cover and refrigerate until thoroughly chilled (at least 4 hours or overnight).
7. **Churn in Ice Cream Maker:**
   - Once chilled, pour the cinnamon roll ice cream base into your ice cream maker and churn according to the manufacturer's instructions, typically about 20-30 minutes, or until it reaches a soft-serve consistency.
8. **Swirl in Cinnamon Roll Mixture:**
   - During the last 5 minutes of churning, drizzle the cooled cinnamon roll swirl mixture into the ice cream maker. Allow it to mix evenly throughout the ice cream.
9. **Freeze:**
   - Transfer the churned cinnamon roll ice cream into a freezer-safe container. Cover with a lid or plastic wrap, pressing it directly onto the surface of the ice cream to prevent ice crystals from forming. Freeze for at least 4 hours, or until firm.
10. **Serve:**
    - Scoop the creamy cinnamon roll ice cream into bowls or cones and enjoy the delightful flavors reminiscent of fresh cinnamon rolls!

This recipe captures the essence of cinnamon rolls in a creamy ice cream form, perfect for enjoying as a special dessert or treat. Adjust the cinnamon and sugar levels in the swirl to suit your taste preferences for a more or less intense cinnamon flavor.

White Chocolate Macadamia Nut Ice Cream

Ingredients:

- 1 cup macadamia nuts, chopped
- 6 oz white chocolate, chopped
- 2 cups heavy cream
- 1 cup whole milk
- 3/4 cup granulated sugar
- 4 large egg yolks
- 1 teaspoon vanilla extract
- Pinch of salt

Instructions:

1. **Toast the Macadamia Nuts:**
    - Preheat your oven to 325°F (160°C). Spread the chopped macadamia nuts on a baking sheet in a single layer.
    - Toast in the preheated oven for about 8-10 minutes, stirring occasionally, until they are golden and fragrant. Remove from the oven and let cool.
2. **Prepare the White Chocolate:**
    - In a heatproof bowl, melt the chopped white chocolate over a double boiler or in the microwave in 30-second intervals, stirring until smooth. Set aside to cool slightly.
3. **Make the Ice Cream Base:**
    - In a medium saucepan, combine the heavy cream, whole milk, and half of the granulated sugar (about 6 tablespoons). Heat over medium heat until it just begins to simmer, stirring occasionally. Remove from heat.
4. **Whisk the Egg Yolks:**
    - In a separate bowl, whisk together the egg yolks and the remaining sugar (about 6 tablespoons) until pale and slightly thickened.
5. **Temper the Eggs:**
    - Gradually pour about half of the hot cream mixture into the bowl with the egg yolks, whisking constantly to temper the eggs and prevent them from scrambling.
6. **Combine and Cook:**
    - Pour the tempered egg mixture back into the saucepan with the remaining hot cream mixture. Cook over low heat, stirring constantly, until the custard thickens slightly and coats the back of a spoon (about 170-175°F or 77-80°C on an instant-read thermometer).

7. **Add Vanilla and White Chocolate:**
   - Remove the custard from heat and stir in the vanilla extract and a pinch of salt. Stir until well combined. Gradually whisk in the melted white chocolate until smooth and fully incorporated.
8. **Chill the Mixture:**
   - Strain the custard through a fine-mesh sieve into a clean bowl to remove any lumps. Stir in the toasted macadamia nuts. Place the bowl in an ice bath to cool the custard quickly, then cover and refrigerate until thoroughly chilled (at least 4 hours or overnight).
9. **Churn in Ice Cream Maker:**
   - Once chilled, pour the white chocolate macadamia nut ice cream base into your ice cream maker and churn according to the manufacturer's instructions, typically about 20-30 minutes, or until it reaches a soft-serve consistency.
10. **Freeze:**
    - Transfer the churned white chocolate macadamia nut ice cream into a freezer-safe container. Cover with a lid or plastic wrap, pressing it directly onto the surface of the ice cream to prevent ice crystals from forming. Freeze for at least 4 hours, or until firm.
11. **Serve:**
    - Scoop the creamy white chocolate macadamia nut ice cream into bowls or cones and enjoy the rich, nutty flavors with the crunch of toasted macadamia nuts and smooth white chocolate!

This recipe creates a decadent and creamy white chocolate macadamia nut ice cream that's perfect for any occasion, combining the indulgent flavors of white chocolate with the buttery crunch of macadamia nuts. Adjust the sweetness by altering the amount of sugar or type of chocolate to suit your taste preferences.

Bourbon Pecan Pie Ice Cream

Ingredients:

For the Pecan Pie Filling:

- 1 cup pecans, chopped
- 1/4 cup unsalted butter, melted
- 1/2 cup brown sugar, packed
- 1/4 cup maple syrup
- 2 tablespoons bourbon
- 1 teaspoon vanilla extract
- Pinch of salt

For the Ice Cream Base:

- 2 cups heavy cream
- 1 cup whole milk
- 3/4 cup granulated sugar
- 4 large egg yolks
- 1 teaspoon vanilla extract
- 1/4 cup bourbon (optional, for adults)
- Pinch of salt

Instructions:

1. **Prepare the Pecan Pie Filling:**
   - In a medium saucepan, combine the chopped pecans, melted butter, brown sugar, maple syrup, bourbon, vanilla extract, and a pinch of salt.
   - Cook over medium heat, stirring frequently, until the mixture thickens and becomes sticky (about 5-7 minutes). Remove from heat and let cool completely.
2. **Make the Ice Cream Base:**
   - In a medium saucepan, combine the heavy cream, whole milk, and half of the granulated sugar (about 6 tablespoons). Heat over medium heat until it just begins to simmer, stirring occasionally. Remove from heat.
3. **Whisk the Egg Yolks:**
   - In a separate bowl, whisk together the egg yolks and the remaining sugar (about 6 tablespoons) until pale and slightly thickened.
4. **Temper the Eggs:**

- Gradually pour about half of the hot cream mixture into the bowl with the egg yolks, whisking constantly to temper the eggs and prevent them from scrambling.

5. **Combine and Cook:**
    - Pour the tempered egg mixture back into the saucepan with the remaining hot cream mixture. Cook over low heat, stirring constantly, until the custard thickens slightly and coats the back of a spoon (about 170-175°F or 77-80°C on an instant-read thermometer).

6. **Add Vanilla and Bourbon:**
    - Remove the custard from heat and stir in the vanilla extract, bourbon (if using), and a pinch of salt. Stir until well combined.

7. **Chill the Mixture:**
    - Strain the custard through a fine-mesh sieve into a clean bowl to remove any lumps. Stir in the cooled pecan pie filling mixture. Place the bowl in an ice bath to cool the custard quickly, then cover and refrigerate until thoroughly chilled (at least 4 hours or overnight).

8. **Churn in Ice Cream Maker:**
    - Once chilled, pour the bourbon pecan pie ice cream base into your ice cream maker and churn according to the manufacturer's instructions, typically about 20-30 minutes, or until it reaches a soft-serve consistency.

9. **Freeze:**
    - Transfer the churned bourbon pecan pie ice cream into a freezer-safe container. Cover with a lid or plastic wrap, pressing it directly onto the surface of the ice cream to prevent ice crystals from forming. Freeze for at least 4 hours, or until firm.

10. **Serve:**
    - Scoop the creamy bourbon pecan pie ice cream into bowls or cones and enjoy the rich, nutty flavors with a hint of bourbon!

This recipe captures the essence of bourbon pecan pie in a creamy ice cream form, perfect for enjoying as a special dessert or treat. Adjust the amount of bourbon to your preference for a more pronounced or subtle boozy flavor.

Grape Nut Ice Cream

Ingredients:

- 1 cup Grape-Nuts cereal
- 2 cups heavy cream
- 1 cup whole milk
- 3/4 cup granulated sugar
- 4 large egg yolks
- 1 teaspoon vanilla extract
- Pinch of salt

Instructions:

1. **Toast the Grape-Nuts Cereal:**
    - Preheat your oven to 350°F (175°C). Spread the Grape-Nuts cereal on a baking sheet in a single layer.
    - Toast in the preheated oven for about 5-7 minutes, stirring occasionally, until they are golden and crisp. Remove from the oven and let cool.
2. **Make the Ice Cream Base:**
    - In a medium saucepan, combine the heavy cream, whole milk, and half of the granulated sugar (about 6 tablespoons). Heat over medium heat until it just begins to simmer, stirring occasionally. Remove from heat.
3. **Whisk the Egg Yolks:**
    - In a separate bowl, whisk together the egg yolks and the remaining sugar (about 6 tablespoons) until pale and slightly thickened.
4. **Temper the Eggs:**
    - Gradually pour about half of the hot cream mixture into the bowl with the egg yolks, whisking constantly to temper the eggs and prevent them from scrambling.
5. **Combine and Cook:**
    - Pour the tempered egg mixture back into the saucepan with the remaining hot cream mixture. Cook over low heat, stirring constantly, until the custard thickens slightly and coats the back of a spoon (about 170-175°F or 77-80°C on an instant-read thermometer).
6. **Add Vanilla and Chill:**
    - Remove the custard from heat and stir in the vanilla extract and a pinch of salt. Stir until well combined. Strain the custard through a fine-mesh sieve into a clean bowl to remove any lumps. Place the bowl in an ice bath to

cool the custard quickly, then cover and refrigerate until thoroughly chilled (at least 4 hours or overnight).
7. **Churn in Ice Cream Maker:**
    - Once chilled, pour the vanilla ice cream base into your ice cream maker and churn according to the manufacturer's instructions, typically about 20-30 minutes, or until it reaches a soft-serve consistency.
8. **Add Grape-Nuts Cereal:**
    - During the last 5 minutes of churning, add the toasted Grape-Nuts cereal into the ice cream maker, allowing it to mix evenly throughout the ice cream.
9. **Freeze:**
    - Transfer the churned Grape Nut ice cream into a freezer-safe container. Cover with a lid or plastic wrap, pressing it directly onto the surface of the ice cream to prevent ice crystals from forming. Freeze for at least 4 hours, or until firm.
10. **Serve:**
    - Scoop the creamy Grape Nut ice cream into bowls or cones and enjoy the delightful crunch of Grape-Nuts cereal combined with smooth vanilla ice cream!

This recipe creates a creamy and crunchy Grape Nut ice cream that's perfect for enjoying as a nostalgic treat. Adjust the amount of Grape-Nuts cereal to your liking for more or less crunch in each bite.

Buttermilk Ice Cream

Ingredients:

- 2 cups heavy cream
- 1 cup buttermilk
- 1 cup whole milk
- 3/4 cup granulated sugar
- 4 large egg yolks
- 1 teaspoon vanilla extract
- Pinch of salt

Instructions:

1. **Prepare the Ice Cream Base:**
    - In a medium saucepan, combine the heavy cream, buttermilk, whole milk, and half of the granulated sugar (about 6 tablespoons). Heat over medium heat until it just begins to simmer, stirring occasionally. Remove from heat.
2. **Whisk the Egg Yolks:**
    - In a separate bowl, whisk together the egg yolks and the remaining sugar (about 6 tablespoons) until pale and slightly thickened.
3. **Temper the Eggs:**
    - Gradually pour about half of the hot cream mixture into the bowl with the egg yolks, whisking constantly to temper the eggs and prevent them from scrambling.
4. **Combine and Cook:**
    - Pour the tempered egg mixture back into the saucepan with the remaining hot cream mixture. Cook over low heat, stirring constantly, until the custard thickens slightly and coats the back of a spoon (about 170-175°F or 77-80°C on an instant-read thermometer).
5. **Add Vanilla and Salt:**
    - Remove the custard from heat and stir in the vanilla extract and a pinch of salt. Stir until well combined.
6. **Chill the Mixture:**
    - Strain the custard through a fine-mesh sieve into a clean bowl to remove any lumps. Place the bowl in an ice bath to cool the custard quickly, then cover and refrigerate until thoroughly chilled (at least 4 hours or overnight).
7. **Churn in Ice Cream Maker:**

    - Once chilled, pour the buttermilk ice cream base into your ice cream maker and churn according to the manufacturer's instructions, typically about 20-30 minutes, or until it reaches a soft-serve consistency.
8. **Freeze:**
    - Transfer the churned buttermilk ice cream into a freezer-safe container. Cover with a lid or plastic wrap, pressing it directly onto the surface of the ice cream to prevent ice crystals from forming. Freeze for at least 4 hours, or until firm.
9. **Serve:**
    - Scoop the creamy buttermilk ice cream into bowls or cones and enjoy the tangy and refreshing flavor!

Buttermilk ice cream has a unique tanginess that pairs well with fruit sauces, compotes, or even enjoyed plain for its refreshing taste. Adjust the sweetness level by varying the amount of sugar to suit your taste preferences.

Avocado Ice Cream

Ingredients:

- 2 ripe avocados
- 1 cup sweetened condensed milk
- 1 cup heavy cream
- 1/2 cup whole milk
- 1/4 cup granulated sugar (adjust to taste)
- 1 teaspoon vanilla extract
- Pinch of salt
- Juice of 1 lime (optional, for a bit of tanginess)

Instructions:

1. **Prepare the Avocados:**
    - Cut the avocados in half, remove the pits, and scoop the flesh into a blender or food processor.
2. **Blend the Avocado Mixture:**
    - Add the sweetened condensed milk, heavy cream, whole milk, granulated sugar, vanilla extract, salt, and lime juice (if using) to the blender with the avocado flesh.
    - Blend until smooth and well combined. Taste and adjust sweetness if needed by adding more sugar.
3. **Chill the Mixture:**
    - Pour the avocado ice cream mixture into a bowl. Cover with plastic wrap, pressing it directly onto the surface of the mixture to prevent a skin from forming. Refrigerate for at least 2 hours, or until thoroughly chilled.
4. **Churn in Ice Cream Maker:**
    - Once chilled, pour the avocado ice cream base into your ice cream maker and churn according to the manufacturer's instructions, typically about 20-30 minutes, or until it reaches a soft-serve consistency.
5. **Freeze:**
    - Transfer the churned avocado ice cream into a freezer-safe container. Cover with a lid or plastic wrap, pressing it directly onto the surface of the ice cream to prevent ice crystals from forming. Freeze for at least 4 hours, or until firm.
6. **Serve:**
    - Scoop the creamy and refreshing avocado ice cream into bowls or cones. Enjoy the unique and delicious flavor of avocado in ice cream form!

Avocado ice cream is creamy, slightly tangy, and naturally sweetened by the condensed milk and sugar. It's a great way to enjoy avocados in a dessert that's both satisfying and refreshing. Adjust the sweetness and tanginess to your liking by varying the amount of sugar and lime juice.

Matcha Green Tea Ice Cream

Ingredients:

- 2 teaspoons matcha green tea powder
- 1 cup whole milk
- 2 cups heavy cream
- 3/4 cup granulated sugar
- 4 large egg yolks
- Pinch of salt

Instructions:

1. **Prepare the Matcha Mixture:**
    - In a small bowl, whisk the matcha green tea powder with 2 tablespoons of whole milk to create a smooth paste. Set aside.
2. **Make the Ice Cream Base:**
    - In a medium saucepan, combine the remaining whole milk, heavy cream, and half of the granulated sugar (about 6 tablespoons). Heat over medium heat until it just begins to simmer, stirring occasionally. Remove from heat.
3. **Whisk the Egg Yolks:**
    - In a separate bowl, whisk together the egg yolks and the remaining sugar (about 6 tablespoons) until pale and slightly thickened.
4. **Temper the Eggs:**
    - Gradually pour about half of the hot cream mixture into the bowl with the egg yolks, whisking constantly to temper the eggs and prevent them from scrambling.
5. **Combine and Cook:**
    - Pour the tempered egg mixture back into the saucepan with the remaining hot cream mixture. Cook over low heat, stirring constantly, until the custard thickens slightly and coats the back of a spoon (about 170-175°F or 77-80°C on an instant-read thermometer).
6. **Add Matcha Paste:**
    - Remove the custard from heat and whisk in the matcha paste until well combined. Add a pinch of salt and stir until smooth.
7. **Chill the Mixture:**
    - Strain the matcha ice cream base through a fine-mesh sieve into a clean bowl to remove any lumps. Place the bowl in an ice bath to cool the custard quickly, then cover and refrigerate until thoroughly chilled (at least 4 hours or overnight).

8. **Churn in Ice Cream Maker:**
   - Once chilled, pour the matcha green tea ice cream base into your ice cream maker and churn according to the manufacturer's instructions, typically about 20-30 minutes, or until it reaches a soft-serve consistency.
9. **Freeze:**
   - Transfer the churned matcha green tea ice cream into a freezer-safe container. Cover with a lid or plastic wrap, pressing it directly onto the surface of the ice cream to prevent ice crystals from forming. Freeze for at least 4 hours, or until firm.
10. **Serve:**
    - Scoop the creamy and flavorful matcha green tea ice cream into bowls or cones. Enjoy the unique taste and vibrant green color of this delicious dessert!

This recipe captures the essence of matcha green tea in a creamy and refreshing ice cream, perfect for matcha enthusiasts and those looking to try something new and delicious. Adjust the sweetness and intensity of matcha to suit your taste preferences for a perfect homemade treat.

Caramelized Banana Ice Cream

Ingredients:

- 4 ripe bananas, peeled and sliced
- 1/2 cup brown sugar
- 2 tablespoons unsalted butter
- 2 cups heavy cream
- 1 cup whole milk
- 3/4 cup granulated sugar
- 4 large egg yolks
- 1 teaspoon vanilla extract
- Pinch of salt

Instructions:

1. **Caramelize the Bananas:**
    - In a large skillet, melt the butter over medium heat. Add the sliced bananas and sprinkle with brown sugar.
    - Cook the bananas, stirring gently, until they are caramelized and golden brown, about 5-7 minutes. Remove from heat and let cool slightly.
2. **Make the Ice Cream Base:**
    - In a medium saucepan, combine the heavy cream, whole milk, and half of the granulated sugar (about 6 tablespoons). Heat over medium heat until it just begins to simmer, stirring occasionally. Remove from heat.
3. **Whisk the Egg Yolks:**
    - In a separate bowl, whisk together the egg yolks and the remaining sugar (about 6 tablespoons) until pale and slightly thickened.
4. **Temper the Eggs:**
    - Gradually pour about half of the hot cream mixture into the bowl with the egg yolks, whisking constantly to temper the eggs and prevent them from scrambling.
5. **Combine and Cook:**
    - Pour the tempered egg mixture back into the saucepan with the remaining hot cream mixture. Cook over low heat, stirring constantly, until the custard thickens slightly and coats the back of a spoon (about 170-175°F or 77-80°C on an instant-read thermometer).
6. **Add Vanilla and Caramelized Bananas:**

- Remove the custard from heat and stir in the vanilla extract and a pinch of salt. Stir until well combined. Stir in the caramelized bananas, making sure to incorporate them evenly into the custard.

7. **Chill the Mixture:**
   - Strain the custard through a fine-mesh sieve into a clean bowl to remove any lumps. Place the bowl in an ice bath to cool the custard quickly, then cover and refrigerate until thoroughly chilled (at least 4 hours or overnight).

8. **Churn in Ice Cream Maker:**
   - Once chilled, pour the caramelized banana ice cream base into your ice cream maker and churn according to the manufacturer's instructions, typically about 20-30 minutes, or until it reaches a soft-serve consistency.

9. **Freeze:**
   - Transfer the churned caramelized banana ice cream into a freezer-safe container. Cover with a lid or plastic wrap, pressing it directly onto the surface of the ice cream to prevent ice crystals from forming. Freeze for at least 4 hours, or until firm.

10. **Serve:**
    - Scoop the creamy and caramelized banana ice cream into bowls or cones. Enjoy the rich and sweet flavor of this homemade dessert!

This recipe captures the delicious caramelized flavor of bananas in a creamy ice cream base, perfect for enjoying as a special treat or dessert. Adjust the sweetness by varying the amount of sugar and caramelization of the bananas to suit your taste preferences.

Pina Colada Ice Cream

Ingredients:

- 1 cup crushed pineapple (canned, drained)
- 1 cup sweetened shredded coconut
- 2 cups heavy cream
- 1 cup whole milk
- 3/4 cup granulated sugar
- 4 large egg yolks
- 1 teaspoon vanilla extract
- Pinch of salt
- 1/2 cup rum (optional, for adults)

Instructions:

1. **Prepare the Pineapple and Coconut:**
   - If using fresh pineapple, dice it into small pieces. If using canned pineapple, drain the juice and crush the pineapple.
2. **Toast the Coconut:**
   - In a dry skillet over medium heat, toast the shredded coconut, stirring frequently, until golden brown and fragrant, about 3-5 minutes. Remove from heat and let cool.
3. **Make the Ice Cream Base:**
   - In a medium saucepan, combine the heavy cream, whole milk, and half of the granulated sugar (about 6 tablespoons). Heat over medium heat until it just begins to simmer, stirring occasionally. Remove from heat.
4. **Whisk the Egg Yolks:**
   - In a separate bowl, whisk together the egg yolks and the remaining sugar (about 6 tablespoons) until pale and slightly thickened.
5. **Temper the Eggs:**
   - Gradually pour about half of the hot cream mixture into the bowl with the egg yolks, whisking constantly to temper the eggs and prevent them from scrambling.
6. **Combine and Cook:**
   - Pour the tempered egg mixture back into the saucepan with the remaining hot cream mixture. Cook over low heat, stirring constantly, until the custard thickens slightly and coats the back of a spoon (about 170-175°F or 77-80°C on an instant-read thermometer).
7. **Add Vanilla and Rum (if using):**

- Remove the custard from heat and stir in the vanilla extract, pinch of salt, and rum (if using). Stir until well combined.

8. **Chill the Mixture:**
   - Strain the custard through a fine-mesh sieve into a clean bowl to remove any lumps. Stir in the crushed pineapple and toasted coconut. Place the bowl in an ice bath to cool the custard quickly, then cover and refrigerate until thoroughly chilled (at least 4 hours or overnight).

9. **Churn in Ice Cream Maker:**
   - Once chilled, pour the pina colada ice cream base into your ice cream maker and churn according to the manufacturer's instructions, typically about 20-30 minutes, or until it reaches a soft-serve consistency.

10. **Freeze:**
    - Transfer the churned pina colada ice cream into a freezer-safe container. Cover with a lid or plastic wrap, pressing it directly onto the surface of the ice cream to prevent ice crystals from forming. Freeze for at least 4 hours, or until firm.

11. **Serve:**
    - Scoop the creamy and tropical pina colada ice cream into bowls or cones. Enjoy the refreshing combination of pineapple and coconut flavors!

This recipe captures the essence of a pina colada in ice cream form, perfect for a summer treat or any time you want to indulge in a tropical dessert. Adjust the sweetness by varying the amount of sugar to suit your taste preferences.

Peanut Butter and Jelly Ice Cream

Ingredients:

- 1 cup smooth peanut butter
- 1/2 cup granulated sugar
- 2 cups heavy cream
- 1 cup whole milk
- 4 large egg yolks
- 1 teaspoon vanilla extract
- Pinch of salt
- 1/2 cup jelly or jam of your choice (strawberry, raspberry, etc.)

Instructions:

1. **Prepare the Peanut Butter Mixture:**
   - In a medium bowl, whisk together the smooth peanut butter and granulated sugar until smooth and well combined. Set aside.
2. **Make the Ice Cream Base:**
   - In a medium saucepan, combine the heavy cream, whole milk, and half of the peanut butter mixture (about 1/2 cup). Heat over medium heat until it just begins to simmer, stirring occasionally. Remove from heat.
3. **Whisk the Egg Yolks:**
   - In a separate bowl, whisk together the egg yolks until pale and slightly thickened.
4. **Temper the Eggs:**
   - Gradually pour about half of the hot cream mixture into the bowl with the egg yolks, whisking constantly to temper the eggs and prevent them from scrambling.
5. **Combine and Cook:**
   - Pour the tempered egg mixture back into the saucepan with the remaining hot cream mixture. Cook over low heat, stirring constantly, until the custard thickens slightly and coats the back of a spoon (about 170-175°F or 77-80°C on an instant-read thermometer).
6. **Add Vanilla and Salt:**
   - Remove the custard from heat and stir in the vanilla extract and a pinch of salt. Stir until well combined.
7. **Chill the Mixture:**
   - Strain the custard through a fine-mesh sieve into a clean bowl to remove any lumps. Stir in the remaining peanut butter mixture until smooth. Place

the bowl in an ice bath to cool the custard quickly, then cover and refrigerate until thoroughly chilled (at least 4 hours or overnight).
8. **Churn in Ice Cream Maker:**
    - Once chilled, pour the peanut butter ice cream base into your ice cream maker and churn according to the manufacturer's instructions, typically about 20-30 minutes, or until it reaches a soft-serve consistency.
9. **Swirl in Jelly or Jam:**
    - During the last few minutes of churning, add spoonfuls of jelly or jam to the ice cream maker, swirling gently to incorporate it into the ice cream but leaving streaks for a marbled effect.
10. **Freeze:**
    - Transfer the churned peanut butter and jelly ice cream into a freezer-safe container. Cover with a lid or plastic wrap, pressing it directly onto the surface of the ice cream to prevent ice crystals from forming. Freeze for at least 4 hours, or until firm.
11. **Serve:**
    - Scoop the creamy and flavorful peanut butter and jelly ice cream into bowls or cones. Enjoy the nostalgic combination of peanut butter and jelly in a cool and creamy dessert!

This recipe creates a delicious peanut butter and jelly ice cream that's perfect for indulging in childhood memories or simply enjoying a unique twist on a classic flavor combination. Adjust the sweetness by varying the amount of sugar and jelly/jam to suit your taste preferences.

Coconut Lime Ice Cream

Ingredients:

- 2 cans (13.5 oz each) full-fat coconut milk
- 1 cup granulated sugar
- Zest of 2 limes
- 1/2 cup fresh lime juice (about 4-5 limes)
- 1 teaspoon vanilla extract
- Pinch of salt

Instructions:

1. **Prepare the Ice Cream Base:**
   - In a medium saucepan, combine the coconut milk and granulated sugar. Heat over medium heat, stirring occasionally, until the sugar has dissolved and the mixture is smooth.
2. **Add Lime Zest and Juice:**
   - Stir in the lime zest and lime juice. Continue to heat the mixture for another 5 minutes, stirring occasionally to infuse the flavors. Remove from heat.
3. **Chill the Mixture:**
   - Pour the coconut lime mixture into a bowl. Stir in the vanilla extract and a pinch of salt. Place the bowl in an ice bath to cool the mixture quickly, then cover and refrigerate until thoroughly chilled (at least 4 hours or overnight).
4. **Churn in Ice Cream Maker:**
   - Once chilled, pour the coconut lime ice cream base into your ice cream maker and churn according to the manufacturer's instructions, typically about 20-30 minutes, or until it reaches a soft-serve consistency.
5. **Freeze:**
   - Transfer the churned coconut lime ice cream into a freezer-safe container. Cover with a lid or plastic wrap, pressing it directly onto the surface of the ice cream to prevent ice crystals from forming. Freeze for at least 4 hours, or until firm.
6. **Serve:**
   - Scoop the creamy and tangy coconut lime ice cream into bowls or cones. Enjoy the tropical and refreshing flavors!

This recipe captures the bright flavors of coconut and lime in a creamy and luxurious ice cream. It's perfect for hot summer days or anytime you crave a taste of the tropics. Adjust the sweetness and tanginess by varying the amount of sugar and lime juice according to your preference.

Honey Lavender Ice Cream

Ingredients:

- 2 cups heavy cream
- 1 cup whole milk
- 1/2 cup honey
- 2 tablespoons dried culinary lavender buds
- 4 large egg yolks
- 1/2 cup granulated sugar
- Pinch of salt

Instructions:

1. **Infuse the Milk and Cream:**
    - In a medium saucepan, combine the heavy cream, whole milk, honey, and dried lavender buds. Heat over medium heat until it just begins to simmer, stirring occasionally. Remove from heat and let the lavender steep for about 20 minutes to infuse the flavors.
2. **Strain the Mixture:**
    - After steeping, strain the lavender buds from the mixture using a fine-mesh sieve or cheesecloth. Press gently to extract as much flavor as possible.
3. **Make the Ice Cream Base:**
    - In a separate bowl, whisk together the egg yolks, granulated sugar, and a pinch of salt until pale and slightly thickened.
4. **Temper the Eggs:**
    - Gradually pour about half of the warm cream mixture into the bowl with the egg yolks, whisking constantly to temper the eggs and prevent them from scrambling.
5. **Combine and Cook:**
    - Pour the tempered egg mixture back into the saucepan with the remaining warm cream mixture. Cook over low heat, stirring constantly, until the custard thickens slightly and coats the back of a spoon (about 170-175°F or 77-80°C on an instant-read thermometer). Do not let it boil.
6. **Chill the Mixture:**
    - Strain the custard through a fine-mesh sieve into a clean bowl to remove any bits of egg or lavender. Place the bowl in an ice bath to cool the custard quickly, then cover and refrigerate until thoroughly chilled (at least 4 hours or overnight).

7. **Churn in Ice Cream Maker:**
   - Once chilled, pour the honey lavender ice cream base into your ice cream maker and churn according to the manufacturer's instructions, typically about 20-30 minutes, or until it reaches a soft-serve consistency.
8. **Freeze:**
   - Transfer the churned honey lavender ice cream into a freezer-safe container. Cover with a lid or plastic wrap, pressing it directly onto the surface of the ice cream to prevent ice crystals from forming. Freeze for at least 4 hours, or until firm.
9. **Serve:**
   - Scoop the creamy and aromatic honey lavender ice cream into bowls or cones. Enjoy the delicate floral notes and sweetness of this homemade dessert!

This recipe yields a beautifully fragrant and creamy honey lavender ice cream that's perfect for enjoying on its own or paired with fresh berries for a delightful summer treat. Adjust the intensity of lavender flavor by steeping longer or using less lavender buds, according to your taste preferences.

Blackberry Cobbler Ice Cream

Ingredients:

- 2 cups fresh or frozen blackberries
- 1/4 cup granulated sugar
- 2 tablespoons lemon juice
- 2 cups heavy cream
- 1 cup whole milk
- 3/4 cup granulated sugar
- 4 large egg yolks
- 1 teaspoon vanilla extract
- Pinch of salt
- 1 cup crumbled cobbler topping (store-bought or homemade)

Instructions:

1. **Prepare the Blackberry Compote:**
   - In a saucepan, combine the blackberries, 1/4 cup sugar, and lemon juice. Cook over medium heat, stirring occasionally, until the blackberries break down and release their juices, about 10-15 minutes. Remove from heat and let cool slightly.
2. **Make the Ice Cream Base:**
   - In a medium saucepan, combine the heavy cream, whole milk, and half of the granulated sugar (about 6 tablespoons). Heat over medium heat until it just begins to simmer, stirring occasionally. Remove from heat.
3. **Whisk the Egg Yolks:**
   - In a separate bowl, whisk together the egg yolks and the remaining sugar (about 6 tablespoons) until pale and slightly thickened.
4. **Temper the Eggs:**
   - Gradually pour about half of the hot cream mixture into the bowl with the egg yolks, whisking constantly to temper the eggs and prevent them from scrambling.
5. **Combine and Cook:**
   - Pour the tempered egg mixture back into the saucepan with the remaining hot cream mixture. Cook over low heat, stirring constantly, until the custard thickens slightly and coats the back of a spoon (about 170-175°F or 77-80°C on an instant-read thermometer).
6. **Add Vanilla and Salt:**

- Remove the custard from heat and stir in the vanilla extract and a pinch of salt. Stir until well combined.

7. **Chill the Mixture:**
   - Strain the custard through a fine-mesh sieve into a clean bowl to remove any lumps. Place the bowl in an ice bath to cool the custard quickly, then cover and refrigerate until thoroughly chilled (at least 4 hours or overnight).

8. **Churn in Ice Cream Maker:**
   - Once chilled, pour the ice cream base into your ice cream maker and churn according to the manufacturer's instructions, typically about 20-30 minutes, or until it reaches a soft-serve consistency.

9. **Assemble the Ice Cream:**
   - During the last few minutes of churning, add spoonfuls of the blackberry compote and crumbled cobbler topping to the ice cream maker, swirling gently to incorporate them into the ice cream.

10. **Freeze:**
    - Transfer the churned blackberry cobbler ice cream into a freezer-safe container. Cover with a lid or plastic wrap, pressing it directly onto the surface of the ice cream to prevent ice crystals from forming. Freeze for at least 4 hours, or until firm.

11. **Serve:**
    - Scoop the creamy and fruity blackberry cobbler ice cream into bowls or cones. Enjoy the combination of blackberries and cobbler topping in every bite!

This recipe captures the essence of blackberry cobbler in a creamy and delicious ice cream. It's perfect for dessert lovers who enjoy the flavors of homemade cobblers in a refreshing frozen form. Adjust the sweetness by varying the amount of sugar in the blackberry compote to suit your taste preferences.

Bacon Maple Ice Cream

Ingredients:

- 6 slices bacon
- 1 cup maple syrup
- 2 cups heavy cream
- 1 cup whole milk
- 4 large egg yolks
- 1/2 cup granulated sugar
- 1 teaspoon vanilla extract
- Pinch of salt

Instructions:

1. **Cook the Bacon:**
   - In a skillet over medium heat, cook the bacon until crispy. Remove from the skillet, drain on paper towels, and let cool. Once cooled, chop or crumble the bacon into small pieces. Set aside.
2. **Prepare the Maple Syrup Mixture:**
   - In a small saucepan, heat the maple syrup over low heat until warm. Remove from heat and let cool slightly.
3. **Make the Ice Cream Base:**
   - In a medium saucepan, combine the heavy cream, whole milk, and half of the granulated sugar (about 1/4 cup). Heat over medium heat until it just begins to simmer, stirring occasionally. Remove from heat.
4. **Whisk the Egg Yolks:**
   - In a separate bowl, whisk together the egg yolks and the remaining sugar (about 1/4 cup) until pale and slightly thickened.
5. **Temper the Eggs:**
   - Gradually pour about half of the hot cream mixture into the bowl with the egg yolks, whisking constantly to temper the eggs and prevent them from scrambling.
6. **Combine and Cook:**
   - Pour the tempered egg mixture back into the saucepan with the remaining hot cream mixture. Cook over low heat, stirring constantly, until the custard thickens slightly and coats the back of a spoon (about 170-175°F or 77-80°C on an instant-read thermometer). Do not let it boil.
7. **Add Vanilla and Salt:**

- Remove the custard from heat and stir in the vanilla extract and a pinch of salt. Stir until well combined.
8. **Chill the Mixture:**
   - Strain the custard through a fine-mesh sieve into a clean bowl to remove any lumps. Stir in the warmed maple syrup until well combined. Place the bowl in an ice bath to cool the custard quickly, then cover and refrigerate until thoroughly chilled (at least 4 hours or overnight).
9. **Churn in Ice Cream Maker:**
   - Once chilled, pour the bacon maple ice cream base into your ice cream maker and churn according to the manufacturer's instructions, typically about 20-30 minutes, or until it reaches a soft-serve consistency.
10. **Add Crumbled Bacon:**
    - During the last few minutes of churning, add the crumbled bacon pieces to the ice cream maker, stirring gently to incorporate them into the ice cream.
11. **Freeze:**
    - Transfer the churned bacon maple ice cream into a freezer-safe container. Cover with a lid or plastic wrap, pressing it directly onto the surface of the ice cream to prevent ice crystals from forming. Freeze for at least 4 hours, or until firm.
12. **Serve:**
    - Scoop the creamy and indulgent bacon maple ice cream into bowls or cones. Enjoy the unique combination of sweet maple syrup and savory bacon in a frozen dessert!

This recipe offers a delightful twist on traditional ice cream flavors, combining the richness of maple syrup with the savory crunch of bacon. Adjust the sweetness and intensity of maple flavor according to your taste preferences for a perfect balance of sweet and salty.

www.ingramcontent.com/pod-product-compliance
Lightning Source LLC
LaVergne TN
LVHW081602060526
838201LV00054B/2025